With best Wishes

Tom

Thanks for the help over the
years and the friendship.

CHRISTMAS TO ANYTIME

Christmas To Anytime

by

RONALD HOW

The Memoir Club

© Ronald How 2004

First published in 2004 by
The Memoir Club
Stanhope Old Hall
Stanhope
Weardale
County Durham

British Library Cataloguing in
Publication Data.
A catalogue record for this book
is available from the
British Library.

ISBN: 1 84104 093 2

Typeset by George Wishart & Associates, Whitley Bay.
Printed by CPI Bath.

To my father, whose perseverance made this book possible, and to my wife, Brenda.

Acknowledgements

*I would like to thank my friends
Jenny Turk, Katharine Matthews and
David Way for their help and suggestions.*

Contents

Chapter 1 Early Days 1

Chapter 2 Play 16

Chapter 3 School 22

Chapter 4 340 Berkhampstead Road 1934-1941 27

Chapter 5 The War Years 34

Chapter 6 Ron How, Carter 43

Chapter 7 The Move 50

Chapter 8 My Time in the Royal Air Force 59

Chapter 9 The Start of the Turkey Industry 66

Chapter 10 Land 76

Chapter 11 Feeding Turkeys 84

Chapter 12 Rearing Turkeys 94

Chapter 13 Breeding Turkeys 108

Chapter 14 Turkey for the Table 117

Appendix I Treasured Turkey Years 130

Appendix II 145

Illustrations

The author's father, M. D. How 2

Pocock egg boxes 11

At grave of Chesham soldier 24

Great-grandmother in doorway of her shop, 1900 28

Breeding birds in the wood (1946-8) 68

The author, on the left, with his father 70

28th day – the chicks have hatched 72

Turkey heart used in medical research at Charing Cross
    Hospital Medical School 83

The author with Bob Pauling 87

Vitamealo concentrate being added to the
    mixing machine 91

Feeding fattening birds, 1951 92

Motley brooders 95

Motley brooders with extensions 96

Hay box 97

Aluminium sheet insulation 99

Home-made brooder and food trough 100

Free-range turkeys in the 1950s 104

Turkey hens with canvas saddles 109

A breeding pen in 1951 110

Bird-operated nesting boxes 111

The author and his father with white and bronze
    breeding males 116

Turkeys for the table – early 1960s 119

A 'flavour full' turkey 123

Turkey portions 125

A white male turkey 128

CHAPTER 1

Early Days

MY FATHER, M. D. How, worked for May Roberts, Manufacturing Chemist, in London and as manager in Dublin from 1921 until his return to England in 1929. He then worked in London in the wholesale perfume trade. He started keeping chickens and ducks in 1934 as a hobby whilst still working in London.

He used to do the morning chores before catching a train to London; on his return there were eggs to collect and feeding to do. Of course, the numbers were not great, about fifty hens and ten or so ducks. To help with the feeding and egg collection, I used to have my own bucket which would carry about a gallon of water and was not very heavy.

Whilst hobby farming, an uncle bet him that he could not rear turkeys. These were notorious for being excessively difficult to rear, the success rate rarely reaching 50 per cent reared to Christmas. Rising to this challenge, he went to Wrights of Germain Street, in Chesham, who were millers and grain chandlers, where he bought the feed for his present enterprise. There he purchased eighteen turkey eggs, which he placed under three broody hens to incubate for twenty-eight days, seven days longer than chickens eggs' take. All hatched and were successfully reared to Christmas, the first and last time we ever hatched and reared 100 per cent, but more about the rearing of turkeys later.

One day, my father found on his desk four directives, from four members of the board of directors, each giving different instructions. These he pinned together and sent to the

The author's father, M. D. How.

chairman, asking if the board could unify its policy. They did and he was sacked. Work was not easy to find in the 1930s, so he turned his hobby into his business. With his mother's help, he arranged a £500 overdraft, guaranteed by her, and rented from a cousin two fields in Missenden Road, half a mile from Chesham, the rent being the manure left on the ground by the birds.

St Dunstan, the training centre for the 1914-18 war blind, was closing down their poultry training farm at Kings Langley and at the sale he made a successful bid for the wire netting and posts from all the pens. He also bid for three wooden poultry houses thirty feet by fourteen feet in size, which was large in those days. This, however, entailed cycling from Chesham to Kings Langley, about eight miles each way, to take down the netting, roll it up, lift the posts and pile them up ready for collection. Dismantling the sheds, however, required three people who could only be found on a Saturday afternoon, as the working week of fifty hours also included Saturday until noon. The sheds were in twenty-six sections but with no floors. When this was completed, a lorry was hired from Mr Wingrove of Hyde Heath to transport the lot to Chesham. As far as I remember this took over a month to complete.

The three sheds were mounted about one foot off the ground, using four-inch drain pipes set in and filled with concrete. Wooden blocks in the top provided a fixing for the wooden floors. Mounting the floors off the ground prevented rats also enjoying a dry and safe home, as there was room for the dog to move under the floors and disturb any unwanted boarders.

Tongued and grooved boards were used for the floors. I had my own hammer and helped drive the nails in and to this day I can still hear my uncle, who was a master carpenter, asking in no uncertain terms why I wanted to choke my hammer.

'What are you doing holding the handle right up by the head? Why do you think they give you a long handle? They want you to use it. Now, hold it down at the end and let the hammer head do the work.'

Each floor cost more than the three sheds combined. One was used to house the winter-laying hens, one as a food store and one for egg packing, storage and later as an incubator room. An engineering friend made a post driver, which enabled one person to drive the netting posts into the ground, without assistance. It was constructed from four pieces of oak, three inches by three quarters of an inch by thirty inches long, screwed and banded together. Hot lead was poured into the bottom quarter. We still had this when the farm was sold in 1999!

A line marked the fence boundary and a crowbar was used to make a starter hole for the posts. This area of Buckinghamshire is well known for its flints, sometimes referred to as Bucks Diamonds, making the use of the crowbar essential. The posts were placed nine feet apart, a short nail was tacked into the post near the top and the netting was hooked on this temporarily. Then, starting at one end, the netting was fastened to the posts with staples. These were not driven right in so that they could easily be removed. The bottom of the wire was pegged down with wood pegs at three-foot intervals to keep the hens in and to try to deter the fox.

There was no mains water or electricity available but luckily the average water table was around fifteen feet below ground level. A pointed end was fitted to a one and half inch diameter water pipe, which had entry holes bored in the lower five feet. This was then driven by hand to a depth of twenty-five feet, in five-foot lengths, using a wooden mallet. A hand pump was fitted and pumping commenced. Chesham has a pure aquifer and after an hour's pumping by hand the water ran clear and pure.

Even in 2001, as I start to write this book, the Water Authority has six pumps working twenty-four hours a day to stop the flooding of a local farmhouse, an agricultural merchants in the Vale, the Elgiva Theatre and Sainsbury's Superstore in the centre of Chesham. The farmhouse is old and in the past they often had to leave both the back and front doors open to allow the river to flow through! Browns, the agricultural merchants, have been flooded at least six times in their history. This year the springs started in late December 2000 and did not recede until September 2001, the longest time in living memory. March until July is the norm. I remember playing Pooh Sticks from the Nashleigh Arms to the British Legion, all of half a mile, in 1937 but that was for a few weeks only.

Pumping and carrying water was a daily chore and continued until 1948 but more about that later. In some years the water level would drop below the bottom of the pipe and water then had to be carried from the river in Germain Street. This was a round journey of two miles with two five-gallon oil drums, which, when filled, weighed fifty pounds each. These drums were carried on yokes, which at the time were still being manufactured in Chesham. This was a twice-daily event whilst the drought lasted.

In the period 1935-1939 it was an uphill struggle to make ends meet. Rhode Island Reds, Light Sussex, and Brown & White Leghorn chickens were used for meat and egg production, as were Aylesbury and Khaki Campbell ducks and I had three geese and a gander. During summer the laying hens were kept in three moveable houses with sixty hens in each. These were kept in the second field but not until a hay crop had been taken. This field sloped and was very stony so its name, Stony Field, was very apt. The hay was cut with a mower pulled by two large horses controlled by one man, whilst a second man was employed full time, sharpening the blades and replacing any broken mower sections. When dry the hay was raked across the hillside into long rows and then, with a horse pulling on either side of the sweep, the hay would be swept to the bottom of the field, where a hayrick was built. This was near the gate, which opened onto the road. Two men would pitch the hay onto an elevator, which was so placed as to drop the hay in the centre of the rick. Here one man would build, a very skilled job. One or two men, depending on the rick size, would feed the hay to him.

The elevator was driven by a horse pulling a pole attached to a large gear, round and round all day. This drove a chain of gears, which eventually drove two chains running parallel, joined by metal bars fitted with spikes, which carried the hay up in a trough. As the rick got higher so the elevator had to be raised. A pole on either side had a pulley at the top over which a wire rope passed down to the top half of the elevator. It was possible to raise the elevator by turning the drum to which the other end of the wire ropes was attached. When I was there, it was my job to keep this horse going as long as hay was waiting to be moved. My pay for that was a ride on the horse, back to the farm, three quarters of a mile in the opposite direction to my home and bed! It was not really such a treat as it was supposed to have been. It was a bareback ride on a sweating horse and, as I only had short trousers, my thighs were soon very sore. I now know that I was not really needed to keep the horse going. It just kept me out of the way.

It was always possible to see where the chickens had been kept the previous year. The crop was much better and larger. This increase was how our rent was collected in the form of a better yield. One year my father lost his pocket watch while helping with the hay making, which was also part of the rent. This was an ex-pilot's watch from the 1914-1918 war. He found it the next year while doing the same job, picked it up, wound it up and off it went, none the worse for twelve months outside.

Winter egg production from October to March took place in the big chicken house, which also had a large outside run. This held about one hundred birds at the start of the winter and the floor was covered with four inches of peat. There were perches and dropping boards running down the back four feet, and nest boxes, windows and access to the grass-run down the front. The rest was exercise and scratching space.

To produce eggs during the short days of autumn and winter it was necessary to lengthen the natural daylight to thirteen and a half hours. With no mains electricity, we had to use acetylene lamps. Calculations were made to ascertain how much carbide would be needed to generate enough gas for the hours required, to an accuracy of plus or minus half-an-hour. These lamps were lit just before dusk and a feed of mixed grain was scattered in the litter, which kept the hens occupied. Three double burner lamps gave enough light and as the carbide was exhausted so the lamps dimmed and the birds made their way to their perches.

These hens were bought from the pheasant-rearing fields after they had reared the young pheasants. The area around Chesham had a number of pheasant farms, including one with the Royal Warrant to supply the Royal shoots. The chickens were Rhode, Sussex or their crosses. These breeds made better mothers than the Leghorn, which were primarily for egg production. These chickens would have been rearing pheasants from early May to September; this gave them a long rest from egg-laying. When they arrived they were put into the laying house and quickly moulted. This is the period when they lose their old feathers and the new ones grow and during this time they do not lay any eggs. This takes five to six weeks but, on good food and light for thirteen plus hours, they soon came back into lay.

Each week the birds were looked over to find any that were about to stop to laying. This was ascertained by handling them, looking at the head where the comb should be large and red; the pelvic bones should be three fingers' width apart. Failing this test meant that they would be killed, plucked and sold as boiling fowl. This was a descriptive name implying that these birds needed to be boiled and not roasted, because of their age. But with dumplings, carrots, swedes and potatoes, they made a very tasty and nourishing winter meal.

Most of the hen eggs were sold retail, packed in cartons of six or twelve, which were sealed with a label that guaranteed that the eggs had been produced and packed on the farm within twenty-four hours of being laid. The date of packing was shown along with the price. Many of these were delivered by me after school, whatever the weather! The shop deliveries were made by my father on a 'Trade' cycle, which had a small front wheel and a home-made, specially sprung, platform to prevent the eggs being cracked. A solid platform fixed to the carrier frame had four tubes fitted near the corners. A similar platform was fitted above with the tubes sliding within the lower tubes; mattress springs were fitted outside the tubes and flexible straps prevented the platforms parting. When stationary the bike had a stand that lifted the front wheel off the ground and kept the platform level and firm. However, when loaded, the rider's weight had to be on the rear of the bike while lowering it off its stand, otherwise it would tip forward with disastrous results. Another problem was caused by the platform hiding the front wheel. When turning, the platform did not appear to turn as quickly as expected, which meant that the handlebars were turned a bit more than normal and, until this was mastered, one could end up on the ground with the bike on top! Any eggs not sold privately or to the local shops were collected, once a week, by Deans of Gubblecote near Tring, who are still trading today under a new name. The man who drove the van had lost a hand but he could still handle a box of 240 eggs and his van with ease.

The ducks were housed within the proximity of the main buildings and, as they laid their eggs early in the morning, they were allowed out to range where they wished. The young Aylesbury ducks were reared in pens, each week's hatch in a separate pen, where they were fattened for killing at ten weeks old and sold to the International Stores along with as many roasters (young cockerels) as they wanted. The Khaki Campbell ducks were kept for their eggs, which were sold for eating.

The turkeys, whilst egg producing, were in four pens. These

ran either side of the hedge between the two fields. Sometimes birds would get out to lay their eggs, by flying over the six-foot high wire netting fence. These nests were difficult to find, and the best way would be to watch the bird when she got out and follow her without being seen. If she had been artful, you could find as many as fifteen eggs in the nest. If she spotted you following her, she would not go to her nest, but would more than likely take you further and further way from the correct place.

Turkeys would start to lay around the tenth of March and stop by the end of May. They would lay around twenty eggs before they wanted to 'go broody', that is, wanting to sit on the eggs that they had laid, to hatch them. If this were allowed to happen, you would find that the poults per turkey would be low. On average only seventeen eggs would hatch and, provided you managed to rear the average 50 per cent, you would end up with eight turkeys at Christmas, less those you had to keep for breeding for the next year. This was not very profitable. To overcome this, and so produce more turkeys per turkey hen, the eggs were collected three times a day to help to dissuade them from becoming broody and to prevent crows and magpies eating them. If any should ignore our gentle persuasion and start to stay on the nest in the evening, they were caught and placed in a specially constructed pen with a wire floor two feet off the ground. Three days in here and they were let out, back into their pen. This was a first-thing-in-the-morning job. If any were so silly as to still be on the nest in the evening, they would spend a further three days in the 'broody' pen.

Talking of 'silly birds', Father always said, 'There's only one thing sillier than turkeys. Anyone silly enough to look after them!' You must have heard the story of the farmer taking his sow in a wheelbarrow to the boar for mating, but what about this? It was common for a pony and cart to arrive with three or four turkey hens loose in the bottom of the cart, with a rope pig net preventing them from flying out. The farmer would have lost his stag (male) turkey, so they would bring the hens to the farm for mating, one mating being enough for one clutch of eggs (twenty). We always had two or three spare males as insurance, should we be unlucky enough to lose any males between November and the end of May. Most farmers keeping turkeys used those that were not good enough to be killed for Christmas; hence some died between Christmas and March when they would be needed to breed. Dad did not subscribe to this practice and, during November, he would select the best birds and put them in pens for next year's breeding. The turkey has come a long, long, way from the pre-war birds, when the hen would weigh around twelve pounds (or five and a quarter kilo) while the males weighed twenty five pounds (or eleven and a half kilo). Today a hen will weigh up to sixteen kilos and the males have weighed as much as thirty-four kilos.

Father had a contract to supply 120 turkey-hatching eggs per week, to a hatchery in Mytholmroyd, West Yorkshire. These were transported by rail in Pocock egg boxes in which each egg had its own pocket of felt of the type used as underlay for carpets. There were thirty eggs to a tray and four trays to a box. Eggs surplus to this were hatched under broody chickens. Two rows of sitting boxes were set out in parallel, with a peg with a string attached, a bowl of water and a place to feed for each hen. The boxes had no bottoms and sat directly on the soil, which helped to provide humidity from the damp soil. With a nest of straw and two or three dummy eggs, we were ready. The hen was placed into the box and after two days, provided that she had settled in, seven or eight turkey eggs, depending on the size of the bird, were then put under her and the dummy eggs removed.

Each morning the bowls were filled with clean water, and maize and wheat were put into the feeders. Then starting from

Pocock egg boxes.

one end, each bird was taken out of the box and one leg was attached to the string. It took about fifteen minutes to complete the round. You now had to remove the string and place the bird back in the same box, as failure to do this could result in the bird giving up sitting. To cover this happening there were always two or three birds sitting on dummy eggs which could then be used to replace those that had given up sitting.

Pre-war, a turkey egg incubation period was between twenty-seven and thirty days. Later on this was stabilized to twenty-eight days by the selection of birds for breeding from those poults (young turkeys) hatched on the twenty-eighth day. Just before the hatching day and before the eggs were piped (which means the shell had a break in it made by the chick within) each hen had a feather wiped between her legs on which was a trace of nicotine sulphate; this was to kill any lice that may have been on the hen. On hatching, the hen and her poults were placed in a coop, a small box with a sloping roof and open front with movable rods that allowed the poults in and out but kept the hen secure. On the first night we would amalgamate the poults from other hatches from the same day so that one hen could look after twelve or so birds. The reason for doing this at night was to prevent the hen killing those she had not hatched.

There were good and bad mothers. The biggest poult loss came from the hens treading on the poults and squashing them. Sometimes a poult would wander into the wrong coop, where it would be attacked. The hen knew that it was not hers and if it did not run away quickly it would most certainly be killed. If the hen managed to get free, she would without doubt take her young through wet grass making them cold and very wet. When this happened it was most important to catch her and return her to her coop, along with her young charges so that they could nestle under her to dry and get warm. When they were six weeks old, the chicks were taken from the hen and placed in pens that had heavy gauge wire netting for the young birds to walk on. In those early days there were no anti-blackhead drugs to cure what was then the scourge of the turkey. Chickens were not troubled by this but could pass it on to turkeys. It was not until the early 1950s that an effective drug against blackhead was produced.

During the summer months, folds were also used to house both chickens and turkeys. The chicken folds were about fifteen feet long with a covered end or ark, and a poop hole that could be shut up at night. As with the turkey folds these had to be moved every day. The chicken folds were heavy and a special tool was used. This consisted of a five foot length of six-inch by one-inch timber with a half-circle made of wood at one end; a rod of steel about twelve inches by half an inch was fixed about two feet up from the outer circle, at right angles. This was placed into a hole in the end of the fold and, by lifting the free end up and over, the fold was lifted and moved sideways. This had to be done twice for each end. When the fold was at the highest point of the lift, the birds would try to reach the fresh grass and one had to be very careful not to catch any under the edge of the fold.

The turkey folds were much lighter, being made from three eighteen-foot and two six-foot lengths of six-inch by one-inch timber and five wooden hoops, specially steamed to a half-circle six feet wide and four feet high. To this wire netting was attached and at one end five feet of roofing felt was held between two layers of netting. One end was also felted but not to the top. This was to allow the wind to pass out, which prevented the fold being blown over. In the other end was a door and just inside a low pail was hung from the ridge board for food and a trough for water fixed in one corner. These were light in weight and could be lifted with eighteen-inch S hooks made from three-eighths-inch rod.

The folds were placed in a straight row with a fold's length between them so that on arrival at one end of their part of the field they could be moved endways on to the unused part and proceed back from whence they came.

I had a gander and three geese. These were allowed to sit on their eggs to hatch them, to produce geese for Christmas. This went well for two years. Then at the start of egg production in their third year, when the gander was getting protective of his ladies, he went for the dog. Well, you can guess who won. The dog was more useful than the geese, as she kept guard and could catch rats and mice. Without a gander the geese were not fertile, so they had to go, as there was no point in replacing the gander. This was a great pity as they fed themselves on grass for most of the year.

The war had not yet started, but men were being called up and volunteering and I saw an advert in the Bucks Examiner for a number of rabbit hutches in which the owner had kept chinchillas for their fur. A bid was made and I became the owner of five four-storey high hutches. I also bought two breeding hutches from a friend of Father's who lived in Germain Street and helped him at weekends. He also sold me two Belgian hare does and a Flemish giant buck and I bought some Dutch does 'in kit' (carrying young) but the young from these did not grow as fast or as large as the other cross so they had to go. There is no place for sentimentality. The fact that they were more docile, and better-looking was not allowed to enter into the equation.

At the peak of production there were one hundred and twenty rabbits of all sizes. These were all fed from the hedgerows with a little bran for the breeding does. The green food was all gathered as part of my work. Clean cabbage leaves would be taken from the waste food collected before it was cooked. During the war the allowance for a doe was twenty-eight pounds of bran per year. The price of a rabbit for eating was seven shillings & six pence, plus a few pence for the pelt, or 37½p in today's money. After the move and the extra work with the poultry I decided to sell the lot, but my mother thought it was too good a money earner to lose and bought them from me. By this time the end of the war was not far way and it was a wrong decision, for the time taken in collecting the food was not as profitable as other work.

There was a time, because we lived in Chesham and not on the farm, that chickens were going 'missing'. We knew who was taking them and where they were sold, but could not prove it. The police advised that we should mark the birds in some way so that it could be proved in court that they were our birds. Father bought a tattooing set that, when pushed into the skin of the bird's wing, made a series of small holes which, after the dye was added, showed up as MDH. While we were tattooing the first birds, our suspect called in and saw what we were doing. We never lost another bird after that.

Soon after the outbreak of war, dad bought two nanny goats and one billy (male) to give us milk for the house and the young poultry. The milking of the goats was another job for me. The nannies were friendly and, most of the time, so was the billy. He would stand beside me having his head rubbed, as peaceful and friendly as one could wish. Then, without warning, he would move his head away and, quicker than one could blink, whack me sideways. Very painful it was. He was not to be trusted in any way. Later on after the move, I was milking one of the goats in a shed where I kept my harness and a saddle that I had saved up enough money to buy (second or more hand) from Mr Cox, our local saddler. When she moved, she bit into the back end of the saddle seat, lifted her head and tore a one-inch strip out of the middle of my saddle.

I had all my harness repairs done by Mr Cox, who was the brother of the headmaster of White Hill School. If it only required stitching, he would say, 'Call in tomorrow,' though it was rarely ready then. About the third time of calling it would be ready. I realise now he never charged me the full amount. The cost to me was between 2d and 9d, the dearer price if a new piece of leather was required.

CHAPTER 2

Play

IN 1935 I CAN remember a little of the Silver Jubilee celebrations for George V. There was a parade from Lowndes Park down to the football meadow where a fête was held. The park pond was dry that year and I remember running across the church end as a short cut. On arrival at the football meadow all children were given a place in the stand along with an aluminium beaker engraved with the King's and Queen's faces and the dates of their reign. A friend of mine still has hers. At the time of the Coronation of George VI, a pencil manufacturer in Bellingdon Road, Chesham, made a propelling pencil with the King's and Queen's faces on and a crown as the propelling part on the top. One of these was given to every school child in Chesham.

In the summer in Lowndes Park there were three boats, which could be hired for 9d for half-an-hour. You had to find the park-keeper to book and hire a boat and he made a note of the time so that he knew when to call you in. Invariably you somehow or other managed to be right at the other end of the lake, as far from the tie-up point as it was possible to be. At weekends the Chesham Prize Silver Band played on the bandstand, the round hard standing that now needs refurbishing.

The winters must have been much harder then than they are now, as the pond used to freeze over every winter and there would be long slides on the ice that we boys used while older people went skating; this would go on for most of January. The Council used to charge one penny to go on to the ice, but it was free on Sundays. During one summer I managed to slip into the pond up to my waist, and I remember going home by the back roads, so not many people would see me, and hoping that I would be dry by the time I arrived home. Of course I was still very damp.

I was the lucky owner of a full-size football and in our spare time we used to play football in the recreation ground by Nashleigh Hill, known as the 'Rec'. One evening, I was leaving with my ball under my arm when someone playfully knocked it out. Unfortunately, it bounced across the road just as a smart sports car came down the hill, driven by a young lady. The car drove right over the ball, which was rather flat when it next came into view at the rear. The car stopped and the driver got out and came over to the group of us and enquired of us whose ball was it. The others, who were all apprehensive as to what to expect, pushed me to the fore. She said, 'Come with me and I will buy you another from Mr Cox.' Not only did I have my ball replaced but I also had a ride in the sports car. Unfortunately I was not old enough to fully appreciate the driver, but she was anyway an 'angel' in my eyes.

We seemed to have certain times of the year when different games were played. We had marbles and dabbers. Dabbers was played with five small flat stones, held first in the palm. You then tossed the stones into the air and caught them on the back of the hand and this continued until all the stones had been dropped. We also had tops that we would whip up and down Berkhamsted Road (the main A416!) These games were played mainly in the springtime. Hopscotch was played on the pavement all the year round. The paving squares were numbered and, starting at number one, you used a stone, or better still, a piece of broken tile, to slide into each square in turn. You then had to hop within the numbered squares to retrieve your stone. If you put your foot down, you had to start again; likewise if you landed on the division between the squares. 'I Acky' was played in Britannia Road where there was a big square. A small chalk circle was drawn in the middle, and the one who drew the short straw would stand in the circle with their eyes closed and count up to ten. Meanwhile the others would have hidden. It was then up to the person in the centre to spot someone and 'I Acky' that one by name. The object was then to get to the centre without being caught. The first one caught then became the one in the centre.

Then there was roller-skating, which we did mostly in Brockhurst Road. At the top of Station Road on the left was the Empire Hall where the grown-ups would roller skate. We kids could only look in through the door when the man in charge wasn't looking. Some kids had iron hoops, which were bowled along the pavement and controlled with a stick, but these seemed to die out before the war came. In season we enjoyed conkers and sledging and any season we played 'four-wheelers'. For this we had a wide plank, or two smaller ones side by side, nailed to a piece of three by two on which the pram wheels, complete with axle, were fixed. The front set was fastened to the main plank with a bolt so that it could be steered. A short piece of rope was fixed to the front for steering and to enable us to pull the four-wheeler along.

The 'Rec' was the favourite spot for four-wheelers as we could pull them up the hill, race down, turn at the bottom and travel along the level piece to slow down. Some four-wheelers had a brake in the form of a piece of wood pivoted at one side which, when pulled up, would rub on the ground and slow you down. The worst thing you could do was to turn too late and too sharply at the bottom. You could overturn or, calamity of calamities, you could buckle the rear wheel. Then it was no more four-wheeling until another old pram could be found.

At the top of the 'Rec' was a steep bank with a hedge that covered the bank from top to bottom. This was a warren of paths where we would play. In the centre was a very large tree, which was a meeting place. We would say 'Meet you at the old oak.' I don't know why, as the tree was ash and is still there today. Also at the top, but on the other side of the hedge and near the road, was 'The Dell' with very steep sides. We had tin trays that we used to crouch on to slide from top to bottom. We rarely hurt ourselves but I think the spoilsports of today's 'Health & Safety' would certainly have stopped us having fun, especially as the main road ran just thirty yards from the bottom of this slide.

It must be remembered that there was no television in those days. We had to make our own fun and we were safe on the streets and byways. We could take a pack of sandwiches and five or six of us would cycle to Marlow to see the Thames, or to Whipsnade to see the wallabies that sometimes would come down to the fence beside the road. Both these trips were up to twenty miles or more. Mums, today, would have to take their youngsters; our mums had neither the time, nor the money nor the transport.

The police were respected, as was people's property. The worst we got up to was 'scrumping' (nipping into someone's field or garden to pick an apple off their tree) or picking up conkers from people's drives for 'conkering', for which, if we got caught, we had a wigging and a clipped ear and, if we were silly enough to tell Mum or Dad, we got another clip around the ear. We knew right from wrong and where we stood. There was none of this 'sue to see how much compensation you can get.' There is too much silly legislation today and not enough pride in ourselves, our town and our country.

I will explain what 'conkering' is all about. When the fruit of the horse chestnut was ripe (September time) we would collect the largest conker and make a hole through it with a meat skewer. A length of string would be passed through this hole and a large knot would be tied at the bottom. Now we were ready to play. One would hold one's conker out in front keeping it steady, whilst the opponent would take a swipe at it with his. The play would then be reversed and this carried on until one conker was broken. The winner would then have a conker known as a 'one'er' and, if he again won with it, it would become a 'two'er'. Should he break one that had a score, then the total score would be added to the winning conker. We used to try baking them in the oven, soaking them in vinegar and keeping them warm in our trouser pockets, but whether any of these dodges worked I do not know.

Some of our games were downright dangerous, like 'bows and arrows' and 'wooden dagger fights'. Bows were made from straight pieces of nut hazel wood about one inch thick with a length of butcher's string tied to each end, while the arrows were made also from hazel but from the new young growth that was very straight and about three-eighths of an inch in diameter. A sharp point was made at the thick end and a notch at the other, to take the bowstring. All this was taken from farmer's hedges but we did not think we were doing anything wrong, and were never admonished.

Wooden daggers were also made from hazel and were carved to look as near the real thing as we could. My brother came home one day after playing in the wood with his friend, with an inch of dagger buried in his face about an inch from his left eye. It had broken off leaving about half an inch sticking out. No blood was to be seen. He was taken to the doctor's and then on to the hospital, where it was removed. He was a very lucky boy indeed.

Cricket was played at school, but after school it was difficult to find enough players to make two teams, so we would play 'French cricket' where the one with the bat had to stand with the bat in front of his legs, which were close together. He could not move his legs until he had hit the ball. He lost when the tennis ball hit his legs. The thrower of the ball then took over the bat.

Another variation was 'tip and run', which was played more

like cricket, only at the slightest touch of the bat by the ball you had to run. You could be 'out' by any of the normal cricket rules.

CHAPTER 3

School

I FIRST STARTED SCHOOL at Newtown Infants School, which was no more than 100 yards from my grandmother's house and shop. I have not many memories of it other than that I first played the triangle and in the last year the side drum. In the September of 1936 our class moved to White Hill School. Mr Stan Cox was headmaster from 1929 until 1951. It is interesting that he had been a pupil in the early days of this school, which first opened on the 3 November 1890. The school was a two-storey building with junior boys upstairs and the senior girls below. Chesham Goods Yard was just below with its coal storage and railway trucks being emptied or filled. There were eight freight lines and some 4,000 tons of freight passed through here a month. Today, Waitrose's car park and the station car park now use this area. Below this was Chesham's Brewery, owned by the Nash family. They supplied most of the pubs around and in Chesham. When the wind was in the west, the smell of brewing was unpleasant.

In 1938 Mr Cox arranged a trip to the rehearsal for the Hendon Air Show. Here we saw the Fairey Battle, a fighter-bomber, dropping bombs on the runway, or more correctly flour bags! This was very pertinent with Hitler and his warmongering. We also saw flying displays, formation flying, a fly-past of Hampden bombers and parachuting.

I cannot remember if it was in 1937, 1938 or both that Sir Allen Cobham brought his flying circus to Chesham. They used a field near the Black Cat at Lye Green for a landing strip. My father treated me to a ten-minute flight in a D. H. Rapid, a twin-engine biplane, over Chesham for ten shillings. I remember seeing logs, which looked no bigger than matchsticks, at one of Chesham's many woodenware factories. This was Howard's factory, which made butter pats and butter stamps, which had a cow or milkmaid carved in reverse. They also made the wooden rulers used by carpenters.

When we landed we spent time looking at a flying 'flea', which was a very small type of autogiro. There was a display of aerobatics and wing-walking by a girl. This is where a biplane has a harness fixed to the top wing and the girl rides there instead of inside the aircraft. You could also, for 7/6d, go up and loop the loop, and be thrown around the sky. Many who tried this were a little green around the gills on landing.

Saturday, 4 August 1939 saw Mr Cox take a group of twenty-seven boys in their last year at his school, me included, to a school camp at Walmer. Ours was not the only school there, and on arrival we were given a hessian palliasse, which we had to fill with straw for sleeping on. This, along with our clothes, had to be carried to the tented field, about half a mile away. Quite a long way, if I remember correctly. Here eight boys were allocated to a bell tent for the week. As I had been in both the cubs and scouts and had been on weekend camps with them, I knew how to go on, keeping one's clothes neat, one's bed comfortable and the tent aired.

On the following Tuesday we boarded the ferryboat called *The Maid of New Orleans* to Boulogne. Here we placed flowers on the grave of a Chesham soldier who lost his life in the First World War. One night while we were at the camp there was a blackout practice and aircraft flew over to see if any light could be seen from the air. We were put on trust not to use our torches or they would be taken from us.

I was in the sports team under the able guidance of Mr Frank Horner, who later was headmaster of a school just outside Aylesbury. I was to meet him again, more than forty years later,

At grave of Chesham soldier, 1914-18 War, August 1939.

as a rotarian of the Thame Rotary Club. He still looked the same. At the morning break we all had a third of a pint of milk, which was given free to all school children. This was started in October 1934 but was one of the things axed by Margaret Thatcher in the 1970s when she was Secretary of State for Education. (The second and much more damaging thing she did was to destroy many of the school playing-fields in one way or another. It was a very shortsighted view, but I doubt that she would agree. Why is it we put up with ministers who think they know best? I thought that they were elected to be OUR representatives, not to satisfy their own personal views.)

The senior class was under the watchful eye of a Mr Rabblin, a very good violinist, whose nickname was Ratty Rabblin. He would applaud, if a pupil at last managed to get the right answer after a struggle, by tapping his thumb nails together up by his own face.

In September 1939 I moved to the senior school in Germain Street. The council was using the school as a centre for the distribution of blankets and extra food for those households taking in evacuees. We boys were used to ferry blankets and food to the houses that had requested help. This lasted less than a week.

My grandmother had one evacuee billeted on her, Alfie by name, about six years old. It was not fair to Alfie or my grandmother. We had three bedrooms, two fairly large and one small one that would only take a three-foot wide bed, pushed right up against the wall, which I and my uncle shared. The other large bedroom was a storeroom for the shop. There was no room for anyone else to sleep upstairs.

This meant that Alfie had to sleep on a couch in the sitting-room between the kitchen and the shop. This was very awkward for all of us. The shop did not close until 7p.m. and in those days a six-year-old had to be in bed and asleep by 6.30p.m. My bedtime was 8p.m. When the powers in charge came to see how the evacuees were settling down, they could see the impossible situation and found Alfie another billet. I do not know what became of him.

When the school settled down we new boys were taken to a room in which there was a piano. As a group we had to sing to find if there were any good voices for the choir. The classroom door opened and in came the headmaster. Mr Thirtell looked over towards me at the back of the class and came walking over, put his ear down near my mouth, looked at me, then walked away shaking his head. I am told even today that it would be much better if I was to shut up, as I sing a half-tone out, though it has always sounded all right to me.

We saw many of our teachers called up and replaced by older men and women. Some days they would be very tired, having been up all night on Air Raid duty. One day we had two German brothers join our class. They had been rescued from

Germany along with their parents. They were only with us for a few weeks before going on to America. It turned out that their father was a German rocket scientist.

CHAPTER 4

340 Berkhampstead Road 1934-1941

DURING THIS PERIOD I lived with my grandmother who owned the grocery and greengrocer's shop on the corner of Addison Road. The shop opened before 7a.m. and closed at 7p.m. Monday to Friday and 9.30p.m. on Saturdays. On Sunday it was closed. In the photograph, taken in the 1900-1905 period, my great-grandmother can be seen standing in the doorway and the name **How** can clearly be read. By 1934 blinds had been fitted over the front window and over the doorway and under here the green groceries were displayed and sold. Inside, many items were stocked, ranging from sweets and tobacco to cheese and vinegar. For this last item you brought a bottle or jug and the vinegar was drawn direct from the barrel and measured by the gill. Sides of both 'green' and 'smoked' bacon were also sold and these, and the large hams, had to be boned before they could be cut on the bacon-slicing machine. Currants and sultanas came in boxes weighing twenty-eight pounds. When a new box was opened grandfather would remove the box top and the greaseproof paper. Next the box was turned out on to a big sheet of greaseproof paper that had been spread out on the table. He then took a basin into which a tablespoonful of golden syrup and half a pint of boiling water had been added. This was poured over the pile of currants or sultanas, which were then stirred. This resulted in a much better looking product, as well as adding a little weight.

The big rounds of cheddar cheese were covered with a clean tea-towel that had been soaked in vinegar. This helped to keep them fresh and in the summer it also kept the flies away. The

Great-grandmother in the doorway of her shop,
340 Berkhamstead Road, Chesham, c.1900.

cheese was cut to the size the customer wanted by a wire fitted to a toggle. Potatoes were kept in and sold from a large wooden barrel; the potatoes were not washed, as are the ones in the supermarkets now. This stopped the potatoes turning green as they were always in the dark. Today, if you look at the flesh just under the skin, you will find that those bought in clear plastic bags have a green tinge. I have always been under the impression that they were poisonous if green.

Woodbine cigarettes were packed in fives, in an open-ended green paper packet for twopence. A packet of Players cost eleven pence ha'penny for twenty. There was a machine outside the shop for after closing-time sales. I had to put a ha'penny for change between the packet and the cellophane outer wrapper, making sure that it could be seen. Customers would not put their shilling in if the ha'pennies were not visible.

Saturday night was bath night, which was in a tin bath in the scullery. My job was to light the fire under the copper which held ten gallons of water. It was used on Mondays to boil the washing in. The fuel used was old cardboard boxes from the deliveries, which were torn up and stuffed into the fire hole.

I always had first bath and was then tucked up in bed. In the winter we had stone hot bottles that were filled with sand. These were put in the oven after the mid-day meal had been cooked. This cooker, or range as it was called, had an open fire and to one side was an oven; there was room on top to boil the pots. All the cooking was done on this and it also heated the room.

During the winter months when there had been a frost, in the morning when we awoke, Jack Frost would have been very busy making beautiful designs on the windowpanes during the night. We had never heard of double-glazing.

My Meccano set taught me a great deal about bracing and strengthening buildings and structures, and my electrical kit taught me about the wiring of light bulbs, switches etc. I also built model airplanes in balsa wood and tissue paper coated with dope to shrink the tissue tight, make it waterproof and strengthen it. When I was ten years old, I won the model-making prize at school and my model plane was on display for three months in Davies the Chemist on the corner of Townsend Road, (now a fast-food shop). Besides being a chemist's, they also sold model kits and were agents for Hornby trains including 'Double O'. All of us school children flattened our noses on the shop window, knowing full well that the goods were far beyond the reach of our pocket money.

On a Tuesday lunchtime I would cycle down to Bones, the newsagents, to collect my copy of *The Hotspur* comic. This I laid across the handlebars of my bike so that I could read as I cycled back. Once, someone had left a small trailer out in the road. They had taken it off the tow-hitch of the car and left it with the hitch on the ground. Not looking where I was going, I rode the front wheel right under the back of the trailer. Fortunately I was only going slowly and no damage was done and at quite an early age I learned not to read and drive! My group of friends each had a different comic so we would 'swap' and so read three or four for the price of one.

Grandmother had an advertising board for the Embassy Cinema (built in 1937) outside the shop. This was paid for by one free ticket for each major film shown. The programme changed twice a week, unless a big film like *Gone With The Wind* was shown, in which case it might be on for two weeks.

One film I remember was about testing to find why planes crashed when flying at high altitudes. Spencer Tracy was the pilot. I can still see the plane spiralling down after the pilot had lost consciousness, through lack of oxygen.

During the summer if the weather were fine, we would all go for a walk after Sunday school. If we were to pick up a stick on these walks, we were quickly admonished and told that we would go to the moon if we collected wood on a Sunday! Occasionally we would go to my great-aunt's, (grandmother's sister), who farmed at Nashleigh Farm. There we would have tea, play games on the lawn and finish up with a singsong around the piano. 'She'll Be Coming Round The Mountain When She Comes' was one. Once, after we had been playing with the tennis rackets, Nancy said, 'Come with me and I'll show you a baby peewit.' We went into one of the grass fields and there we were able to trap one with our rackets just long enough to look carefully at it.

They had a dairy farm and supplied their brother, Uncle Erne. He, with the help of his wife, delivered milk around the houses. My aunt travelled on foot, carrying a milk bucket complete with lid and a gill measure, which was used to transfer the measured milk into the customer's own jug. Uncle had a milk-barrow, from which he used to deliver further away.

A milk barrow had two large wheels and a smaller front steering wheel and could carry one or two churns, of ten gallons each.

At that time there were a dozen or more woodworking factories employing many people. Much of the timber came from the woods around and a lot was carted by horsepower. If the tree was short but with a large girth it would be slung under a special cart that was backed over it; chains were passed under and around it at the point of balance. It was then raised by pulleys and it travelled to the sawmill, one horse between the shafts, with another connected by draft chains to assist in the pulling. If the load were too big, a third horse would be used.

The other type of cart had a front pair of wheels attached to a turntable to which the shafts and horse were connected. Also connected was a long timber about ten inches square, in which holes were bored from top to bottom. The other pair of wheels and axle slid along this timber and were locked into position with strong pins that were passed through the holes on either side of the axle. The position was determined by the length of the trees to be carted.

To load this type, the trees were hauled to the side of the wagon by the horses, butts to the front. A chain was attached to the timber that ran between the two pairs of wheels, under the tree and over the cart to the far side where it was attached to a whippletree (also known as a swingletree in other areas) which was attached to the horse's collar by chains. Posts were placed at an angle for the tree to slide up. The horse was then led forward and the tree slid into position on the wagon. It was prevented from going right over by two upright wooden posts that were placed in holes in the cross shafts for that purpose. This was then repeated until a full load was aboard.

T. T. Boughton's hauled a lot of timber but they used a steam-driven truck to haul their timber wagons, while Jesse

Wright had a petrol-engine one. Both of these could carry three or four times the amount that was possible with horsepower.

Chesham was well known for its brushes; at least five factories were making anything from scrubbing brushes of many types to sweeping brooms and paintbrushes. One just made broom handles. Jesse Wright made the cheap cricket bats and was the biggest woodenware factory in town. During the war a large part of its output was ammunition boxes. One could buy sawn timber for one's own conversion. When we put a second floor in our food store and mixing shed, Jesse Wright supplied us with nine by three-inch green oak joists twelve feet long, which were topped with one-inch thick oak flooring.

A great deal of woodturning was also done, producing fruit bowls, salt and pepper mills, shaving-soap bowls, Manakin cigar boxes, wooden shovels for grain and malt moving, yokes for carrying milk pails and butter pats, moulds and the like.

There were three boot factories, one making army boots, another making safety boots and shoes with steel toecaps. In the seventies one of their boots was to save my son's foot from being crushed. When he came to tip three tons of grain into the reception pit, he moved the hydraulic lever and the trailer shoe crashed down on to his foot. His toes were just grazed and no damage was done except to the boot. He was a very lucky lad. We supplied all our staff with safety footwear, which they had to wear. These are still made in the same factory today.

There was a plaiting works and a pencil factory; handbags and riding saddles were made and there were very many small metalworking units. Parts for the Mosquito fighter-bomber were made during the war. The local Chesham Building Society was first founded in 1845. As all building societies formed earlier have stopped trading, it is therefore the oldest in the world and still going strong. Chesham has the first and oldest Lawn Tennis Club which is also still strong. Then, of course, by no means least, there was us, with the first turkeys produced out of season and in consequence the first freezing turkeys on the farm.

CHAPTER 5

The War Years

BY 1939 THE poultry business was just starting to be profitable, but the dark clouds of war were not far away. It was during August that Mr Knowles from Berkhamsted, who supplied our poultry food, came and asked my father if he would allow him to fill our small food store with grain. It was pointed out that it would not be possible to pay for that amount of food straight away. Mr Knowles replied that he was quite aware of that but we could pay for it as we used it. A very kind and thoughtful man, his help was very much appreciated.

Soon after his visit his 'big lorry' arrived fully laden with five tons of poultry feed. I remember one of his drivers had a pet saying. 'My boy, if you always have a penknife, a piece of string and a shilling, you will never want for anything.' I do not think the shilling would go far in today's world, but I still carry a penknife, and usually a piece of string.

With the outbreak of war, poultry food, along with many other things, was rationed. I know that the monthly allowance for poultry was one-eighth of the average purchased during the previous three months (June, July, and, August). As September, October, and November were our biggest months for food usage you can see how drastic this was to our business. As we had not paid for the five tons from Mr Knowles, it did not count.

First the contract to supply the turkey eggs to Mytholmroyd in Yorkshire was cancelled. So that hen eggs could be rationed, all eggs produced had to go to an egg-packing station. This meant that Deans collected all the eggs we produced, for which they paid wholesale price, and our retail trade had to stop.

The local councils had to allot sites within the town where citizens had to put their household food scraps to be collected. Chesham was shared between Mr Bishop, the local pig farmer, and my father. They had to provide a dustbin with lid, and keep the bins cleared and clean at each site.

So that I could help, Mayo & Hawkes, the local cycle shop in Red Lion Street, still trading today, were asked to make a trailer that could be pulled behind my bike. A square, the size to take a dustbin, was made from one-inch by one-eighth-inch steel, two bicycle wheels and a drawbar. Two u-shaped pieces of metal were riveted together. One end was fixed to the bolt, which held the saddle pillar to the frame; the other had two holes through which a bolt slid to attach the drawbar of the trailer. These had to be emptied three times a week, by me, after school. I was permitted to leave school early when the daylight was short. The round trip was about three miles. On arrival at the farm these scraps had to be cooked, in a copper holding about ten gallons, with a fire underneath – another job for me in my spare time!

The Alfa Lavall steaming copper, which replaced the old ten gallon one, was very much larger. It held about four dustbins full of scraps; four to six gallons of water were put in the bottom, then the steaming plate was put in. This had brackets on the underside to keep the plate just above the top of the water. From the centre a tube extended almost to the top. Holes had been drilled into this from which steam and hot water sprayed into the scraps. A lid was fastened to the top and there was also a handle to tip the cooker forward for emptying. The water was heated by burning leather offcuts, known as shreds, (in Chesham these came from one of the boot factories making army boots so were easy to come by) supplemented with wood.

The pressure cooker had a double steel skin and the removable lid, held on by ten half-inch bolts, was about forty inches high and twelve inches in diameter. A gallon of water was added and a perforated plate placed over this at the bottom, then the fish heads, bones, etc. filled the remaining space. A large type of blowlamp, burning paraffin, provided the heat. This built up steam to a pressure of forty pounds. At this point the heat was removed and the cooker allowed to cool and the pressure to drop before opening. The resulting product was a much-needed supply of high-quality protein, looking like fish paste. This mix had to be fed twice a day as, being damp, it would quickly go sour and then cause problems. It was carried in two large pails on yokes and fed into wooden 'v' troughs with a large wooden spoon made in Chesham!

At that time we had a stag (male) breeding turkey, Solomon by name, who was rather vicious and would attack from behind. He had previously flown up and hit Father in the middle of his back, sending him sprawling on the ground, which made him very wary when Solomon was near. As Father was carrying two buckets full of food on the yoke and with the spoon in his right hand, this stag started to attack from behind. Wary of his last attack and without looking, father swung the spoon round behind him and caught Solomon on the head, knocking him out cold. There was great consternation, for this was a valuable breeding bird that we could not afford to lose. We made a quick run to get a teaspoon and the brandy bottle, his beak was forced open and a teaspoon of brandy was poured down his throat. It was with great relief that we saw his eyes open, and then he managed to get to his feet and staggered off. Whether it was a headache or a hangover that caused the stagger we will never know, but he did not try any more attacks.

My pay for this work was five shillings a week, provided that I bought one fifteen-shilling saving certificate each month. This gave me double spending money every third month.

Kraft had a factory at Hayes in Middlesex where the cheeses were trimmed of the cloth and outer layer before being cut up for sale, on ration, to the retail shops. This provided another good source of protein. One day on a visit to the factory, I saw the rind being removed from the large rounds of Cheddar cheese. There was a bench with what looked like a quarter of a barrel (a barrel cut in half and then cut in half vertically). In the base was a slot with a rotating roller; the half-barrel was inclined at about sixty degrees. The cheese was placed above the slot. This rotated the cheese and the operator held a spoke-shave to the top of the rotating cheese, moving downwards as required. Thus the rind was very quickly peeled away. This rind was sold for pig and poultry feed, again no feed coupons being required. We soaked this in water and when it was soft we would remove the cheesecloth. In doing this, our hands were made very soft and clean.

We were lucky that sometimes we could obtain broken biscuits from Askey's of Aylesbury, of ice-cream wafer fame. Sometimes we could buy damaged potatoes to supplement the rationed poultry feed. Later on, the Tottenham Council started to collect the scraps from boroughs in London, which they cooked and sold as 'Tottenham Pudding' in fifty-six pound sacks. The Government encouraged householders to keep chickens in their garden. To meet this demand we offered six point-of-lay chickens in a battery, which was made on the farm. There was a good demand for these from up to a ten-mile radius. The householders were allowed twenty-eight pounds of 'Balancer meal', so-called as it was to balance the scraps from the house and give a much better ration. Several of these would be delivered at the same time, using Ben Wingrove and his lorry. The chickens would travel in wooden crates along with the battery, drinking bowls and food troughs. A charge was made for delivery. There was a need for replacement hens later on which we supplied, delivered by father on his trade bike.

To help supplement the income and enable him to continue to employ a lad who had been working for him since he had left school, Father took a job as a gardener for two days a week in Little Missenden. The river Misbourne flowed through the garden and, to supplement our own food ration and that of his employer, he would catch trout. No, he was not paid to stand on the bank casting in the traditional manner. He found a five-gallon oil drum, which he cleaned. The bottom was removed and holes were made in the sides and top with a pickaxe. A wire was tied to the handle at the top. This was placed on the bed of the river, with the bottom facing upstream, and the wire was secured on the bank. As this provided a safe, shady spot, with a good flow of water, the trout would spend a lot of time in there. When the menu called for fish, father would just lift it from the river-bed by tilting it forward on to the top, thus keeping the fish in the drum. Most times there would be two or maybe three trout for the taking. Unfortunately, my father had to leave this job as, one evening, on arriving back at the farm, he found the lad he employed to help sitting on one of the costly wooden floors with a brace and bit, busily boring holes through them. It was found that the employee had a tumour on his brain and he died a few weeks later.

My uncle (the master carpenter) used to shoot pigeons with a single barrel .410. As a treat I was sometimes allowed to go with him. But the first noise I made, it was straight back home. I learnt how to move noiselessly, by taking small paces, by not putting my foot straight down but feeling with the foot in case there was a small twig or branch which, if trodden on, could make a noise like a pistol crack. I also learned how to move through a wood without disturbing branches or bushes so that no indication of my presence was seen.

Once when I was in front, (we never ever walked side by side) I heard uncle fall. Turning round, I saw him on the ground by a small bush. He indicated that I was to carry on.

When he caught up with me I noticed the back of his jacket had a slight bulge, which meant he had something in his poacher's pocket. He said that when he slipped over, he found he had landed on a pheasant! If you find a rabbit, hare or a pheasant sitting in a form or shelter and you walk past, provided that you do not turn round and go back to look again, it will not run away. Should you wish to see it again, you must detour and approach from the same direction.

He taught me how to read rabbit runs and where to set the snare to catch the rabbit as it took the next hop. Any new snares, which I purchased from Hampshire's, the ironmongers in the High Street, were buried in sand for three weeks to make sure the brass wire they were made from would lose all of its shine. This made sure that the moon did not warn the rabbit by reflecting off the new shiny surface. The most rabbits we caught on any night was thirty-five, of which the fox had eaten seven. Even with that loss, it was a very profitable night's catch. How do you set a snare? Firstly, you need a strong peg to tie the snare to, next a one year's growth from the base of a hazel bush, the type we used for arrows! Six inches long, a point is made at one end and a notch at the other. These are placed just off the run and in line with the less worn part of the run. The strong peg is knocked firmly into the ground after a groove has been cut to take the string that is attached to the snare. Next, the small peg is pushed into the ground almost up to the run. The loop of the snare is opened to your hand's width (about four inches,) the loop side of where the wire is fixed to the string goes into the notch in the small peg. This is set to hold the snare four inches off the ground with the loop uppermost.

He also taught me how to shoot and never ever to point a gun at anyone, even if you had just taken the cartridges out of it. I was allowed to shoot rats with the .410, and at that time Chesham Town Council would pay 2*d* for every rat-tail taken to their office in the High Street. You had to be there between 10a.m. and 12 noon on a Saturday. A coke fire was always burning in the grate, and the man in the office would stand beside the fire and count the tails, while I took them out of the tobacco tin in which I kept them, and throw them on to the fire. The money was mine, a perk that on a good week could be 2/- or 3/-. I did have the feeling that they would not worry if I missed a week!

By the age of fifteen I was allowed to use father's .22 rifle, which did not make as much noise and had a longer range than the .410. It was dangerous within a mile and, wherever you shot, you had to be sure that the bullet could not travel further than you could see. This meant there were many times when you could not fire.

When I was seventeen, the age you could own your own rifle, I called in at the police station for a licence application form. The sergeant at the desk said, 'I suppose if we don't give you one, you will carry on using your father's as you do now.' They gave me one, or rather they allowed me to buy one. During the war the police ran a dance every Friday night at the drill hall. They used the hall on the first floor, which was a Territorial Army drill hall and .22 rifle range. The Cadet Forces used it for rifle practice. Every boy was expected to be a member of the air, army or navy cadet corps. I was a member of the A.T.C. There is still an Air Cadet Force in Chesham.

Chesham did not have many bombs; however, the local blacksmith lost his daughter when a bomb hit their house near the Embassy Cinema. Ironically, had the air raid warning been sounded, she would have been on ARP duty. This stick of bombs also dropped on Germain Street School, just missing the dental clinic for the schools in the area. It did, however, break a number of school windows. I remember helping to clear up the playground, after which we were sent home for the rest of the day.

An oil bomb landed in the garden of a house in Lyndhurst Road. Luckily, the incendiary device did not go off, which meant that the house was sprayed with oil and a mess made of the garden. I can still hear the whistle the bomb made as it fell. Another stick of bombs dropped across the bottom of Missenden Road from the Bury Farm to the allotments. We saw the plane drop these one Saturday morning, about 11.30a.m. It was a cloudy morning and the pilot just came out of the clouds, released his bombs and returned to the cover of the clouds. As this was just half a mile from the farm, we hopped on our bikes to see what had happened. The bombs had all fallen onto fields, and as no one else had appeared, we had a good look round. We found one that had made a hole about fifteen inches across which my pal went down. With hindsight it was not the thing to do, but luckily he was soon back, reporting that it had made a cave about eight feet down.

Another time they just missed hitting Latimer House. A number fell around Chesham, and one fell near Hyde Heath, killing a number of cows. This was a land mine, a bomb that was dropped attached to a parachute, which prevented penetration and relied on blast to do the damage.

These were all dropped during the Battle of Britain, as was the 'dog fight' we saw one day in September. I was changing, having just arrived home from school. The bombers had just bombed Luton and were returning to base when the RAF engaged them. We could see the bombers with our fighter weaving around in a clear blue sky. During the short time they were in our vision, no plane was shot down. My future wife, Brenda Brown, was machine-gunned by a plane. Luckily she was not hit.

There was little more activity around us until the V1, or Doodle Bug, attacks. We were at Woodlands Farm then and it was one Wednesday afternoon at five to five when one dropped in the garden of The Glebe House at Heath End. My mother, whose shopping day was always Wednesday afternoon, was cycling home and asked someone where it had dropped, only to be told 'The Turkey Farm.' I think my mother's bike must have broken the speed limit that day as she arrived home, flustered and out of breath, to find that, fortunately, it had missed us by a mile. The next day a second Doodle Bug fell a quarter of a mile further on into an empty field, this time at 11.30 in the morning.

A number of our own aircraft made false landings and a regrettable number crashed. At Bovingdon, about four miles away as a plane flies, we had an American B17 or Flying Fortress airfield. The main runway is still there but is not used nowadays. They say one part of this runway is twenty-four feet thick, where a hollow was filled in, but whether this is true I do not know.

I have a painting by John Young, G.Av. A. showing a B17 coming in to land with a field of corn being harvested. One of the people in the painting could have been my wife's father, as they farmed the land under the flight path.

CHAPTER 6

Ron How, Carter

THE COLLECTION of scraps from the town was getting more than we could manage on our combined bicycles and, to focus our minds further, the Army had requisitioned Latimer House and its grounds to build an army camp. They were looking for someone to collect the kitchen and dining-room waste, six days a week. As you can well imagine, this was a lot of very good food, which would enable us to increase the number of birds that we could keep. We needed a much larger form of transport to cope with this. Inquiries were made as to where a pony and cart could be found, should we be granted the contract by the army. There was no way my father could afford to buy the pony and cart and he asked me if I would cash in my savings certificates that had been bought for me at one per month for the first three years of my life. In return he would hire it from me at two pounds ten shillings a week, but I would have to pay for all the horse food, harness repairs and shoeing.

The contract with the army was given to us with a starting date. A Mr Delaney, who lived at Cannon Mill and was an Irish wheeler-dealer, had found a pony and cart in London. The pony was a wee bit thin but, coming from London and with a war on, it was to be expected. The cart was a typical London-type, with iron wheel bands and small high sides which made it difficult to lift the dustbins over when full. The brake had two wooden blocks which, when the pedal was pushed with one's foot, rubbed on the rear steel tyres. If the hill was steep or long, there was an iron shoe that fitted under the rear nearside wheel to prevent it turning. It also stopped the tyre wearing. A chain, fitted to the underside of the floor of the cart, prevented the skid going too far under the wheel; at the bottom of a hill one had to stop, back the cart off the skid, pick it up and hang it up.

This cart was hard on both the pony and the carter, so I made enquiries about a better cart. Mr Tomlin, the local coachbuilder, said he could build one if I could find the materials. I found that a neighbour had a 1926 Peugeot car, which he sold to me for six pounds. I managed, with the pony's help, to tow the car the short distance to our farm. Then it was a dismantling job. To start with, the wheels had to come off. This required jacking up the car to enable this job to be done. I had just started jacking one wheel up when my uncle, who farmed the rest of the land we were on, appeared. 'What do you think you're doing?' he enquired. My reply was 'Taking it to pieces, Uncle.'

'Well, stop mucking about and go and find me a sack.'

Wrapping the sack around the bumper, he said, 'Have you got all your bricks ready?'

He then bent down, took hold of the bumper and lifted the front end, complete with engine, off the ground. 'Make sure you have the bricks safely stacked under the axle, then we will do the rear for you.'

Over the next few weeks all my spare time was spent taking the car apart. (Today that car would have been a collector's item.) When this was completed, the wheels and axles, along with what planks I could scrounge from various people, were loaded on to the old cart and taken to Mr Tomlin at his Bellingdon Road workshop in Chesham.

Another example of my uncle's strength was shown one day when he was driving his milk float, a small lorry, and one tyre went flat. What did he do? He laid the spare beside the offending wheel, took the spanner and loosened the wheel nuts, then lifted up the float with one hand and removed the nuts. He then replaced the wheel, tightened the nuts, lowered the float to the ground and was on his way in less than five minutes.

When a man went to him for a job, he would have a sack of wheat, a total weight of 256 pounds or 116 kilos, waiting on a ledge by the back door. The applicant had to carry this across the farmyard and up an almost vertical ladder – not an easy thing to do. Failure resulted in the retort 'You're no bloody good to me. On your way.'

There is a tale in the family that a great uncle could lift a barrel of beer and drink from the bunghole. Now a barrel holds forty gallons or 400 pounds. Add to that the weight of the barrel and that's over 500 pounds or 226 kilos!

I have an invoice dated 7 September 1812, from Joseph How, Brewer, Church Street, Chesham – my great-great-great-grandfather. The house is still standing today. The invoice for nine gallons of XXX Ale – 9/-(nine shillings) equals less than one new penny a pint!

When I received word from Mr Tomlin that my new cart was ready for collection, I took the pony down, with his harness on, to collect it. I do not remember how much it cost, but with both a foot brake and a handbrake acting on both rear wheels, rubber inflatable tyres and a much lower loading height, it was a great improvement, making both the pony's and my job much easier.

Paddy, as my first pony was called, was finding working six days a week a bit too much for him, so I asked Mr Delaney if he could find a younger and slightly larger pony for me. But before we leave Paddy, I must report on one of his bad points. As I said, he came out of London where he had worked for a costermonger's and was only used to hard roads, not soft grass. I always had to lead him by the head, the only way you could control him, until he was on the hard road. Once, and only once, he managed to snatch the reins out of my grasp and charged out on to the road. He proceeded to travel at a gallop down the road towards Chesham. I followed behind, picking up the dustbin lids along the way. Fortunately, our neighbouring farmer was coming up the road and saw Paddy coming down towards him at full gallop. He pulled his horse and cart across the road, blocking Paddy's progress. When I caught up, Paddy was tied to a very large tree, his sides heaving. After I had thanked Mr Woodly profusely, I rearranged the dustbins, replaced the lids, untied a now subdued Paddy and restarted my day.

So, at the age of thirteen years, I became a carter in my own right and said goodbye to the pulling of the trailer behind my bike or using a sledge when the snow was too deep to cycle. No more walking two miles with water from the river in times of drought. The only downside I found was having to sit on the cart during the cold weather, without any form of shelter. On the bike you were kept warm pedalling.

I left school at Christmas 1941, aged fourteen, and for six days a week, come rain, frost, sun or snow, I made the trip to Latimer, six miles each way. The quickest the job could be done was three and a quarter hours. This was totally dependent on how long it took the soldier, who had to meet me, to take the cart into the camp. The nearest I, or any one else for that matter, was allowed to the camp was about a quarter of a mile. There is a private bridge over the river Chess just below Latimer House and this is where I had to wait. They usually took an hour to return with the loaded cart. At first I spent my time bird-watching. There were kingfishers darting into the river catching young trout fry. Rainbow trout could be seen jumping a small waterfall below the bridge on their way upstream to spawn. Male wrens were building endless nests. They would take their mates round to inspect their handy work, forever hopeful that the latest work would meet with approval and they could get on with the job of rearing a family.

One day two swans were fighting on the piece of land between the main river and a smaller river, which took the water from the mill. I jumped over the fence, grabbed one by the neck as I had done with my geese, put it over the fence into the small river, then drove the other into the main river. It was not until I told my mother what I had done, and she had given me a good wigging, that I realized how lucky I had been.

Sometimes one of the soldiers would come down to see what I was up to and why I was in a restricted area. He would stay and talk for a while. Never once was a hint given what the camp really was, and it was not until well after D-Day that I was allowed inside the camp with a special pass. It was then I found out what it truly was. Most of the kitchen staff, both male and female, were German. The name of the camp was Number One Distribution Centre. Any prisoner who, it was felt, had information that could help the war effort was sent here for interrogation, before being sent to more permanent quarters. Hess was there for a while. Later it became the Joint Services Staff College and, later still, a conference centre, as it still is today.

The person in charge of the mill used to come up every day to the topside of the large waterfall about seventy-five yards upstream from the bridge. I didn't really know why, but I could see him turn a large wheel several turns. Later I found that he, Mr Gilbert, was allowing water, from the lake into which the river Chess flowed, to pass through a turbine to drive the sawmill and corn mill and also to drive a generator to recharge a large bank of batteries that supplied the farm and houses with electrical power. One day when it was pouring with rain, he came down to the bridge where I was sheltering as best as I could. He asked if I would like to come to the mill and shelter. I replied that the pony and cart would be down in a very short while, but could I come the next day. This he said would be all right and proceeded to show me how to get to the mill.

This began a very happy and much drier time. I helped him on his daily chores, for example, sawing oak tree trunks into nine-inch by nine-inch posts eight feet long, from which to hang gates. Other times it could be sawing pine into boards to repair buildings or putting points on round posts for fencing. From the offcuts, boards were made for beehives and honey boxes, called lifts, to go inside the hives, of which he had eight or nine. I also helped to roll oats for the horses and cattle and kept an eye on the very large acid batteries that the generator charged up. Should there be a shortage of water, there was an 'oil engine'. I think it was a single cylinder with a very long stroke, about four feet long, and with a ten-inch piston. The driving-wheel was about four feet in diameter. The cylinder head was heated with a blowlamp and when it was hot the flywheel would be turned, drawing in air and paraffin, and off it would go. I only saw it work once and that was just to make sure it would work if needed.

The whole place was the main maintenance depot for Lord Chesham's estate. Latimer House was supplied with electricity from there before the army moved in, as were all the cottages that the workers lived in. The army needed much more power than could be supplied by the set-up here, and they had a mains supply connected. Mr Smith of Blackwell Hall farmed the farm, the cattle building and surrounding land. His own farm was about a mile up the road towards Chesham. If Mr Gilbert had no job for me, I would help them. During the five years I helped there, I learned a great deal that was useful to me later on at home. I learned, for example, how to prepare straw for thatching. One took the long wheat straw from the trusses that they had been tied in when the wheat was threshed, laid them in a row, cut the ties and then proceeded to soak the straw thoroughly with water. A heavy piece of timber was laid on top and left until the next day. The straw was then raked with a pitchfork to straighten it and remove the dross. The straw was pulled out into small bundles called 'yealms', which was just the right amount for the thatcher to place up the rick. As many yealms as were required to reach the top or ridge were placed in a pile, each yealm being placed at an angle to the lower one, enabling them to be picked out easily by the thatcher. The thatcher would start at the eves, where a tied bundle of straw had been pegged to give a kick to the slope of the first yealm laid in order to shoot the water away from the rick side. Then he would work his way to the ridge, laying each yealm to lap over the lower one, much as tiles are laid on a house. Then string would be pulled over each yealm and tied to a wooden peg driven into the sheaves below, to hold each in place. A 'corn dolly' would be placed at each end of the ridge, depending on their shape; they would be to say thanks for a good harvest, to ensure a good harvest next year, or just as a good luck charm.

CHAPTER 7

The Move

MANY PEOPLE must have wondered why we built our farm on a field with a slope of one-in-four. This is why.

On 27 November 1942, his birthday, my father received a letter from a farmer from Hertfordshire, stating that he had bought the farm and, as we had no legal standing as tenants, would we please vacate the site as soon as possible. To make matters even more desperate, the food ration for the birds did not go with the person but with the property and, to compound our troubles even further, the new rationing period was 4 December. However, the War Agricultural Committee said they would allow the ration to be transferred, if we could find somewhere to go before 4 December. I do not remember much of that week but somehow my father was able to find a field that had not been ploughed and was not subject to a ploughing order. During the war there were ploughing-up orders made on any and every field that would grow corn. My father arranged finance to make the purchase and then cycled over to Stoke Mandeville (eight miles each way) on 4 December, to where the Bucks War Agricultural Committee had their offices, with proof that he had land in the Vale, Chesham. They transferred the food ration to Woodlands Farm, a name we had a week to choose. That week must have been the longest and most traumatic week in my father's life. The field in the Vale was thirteen and a quarter acres, with five acres of woodland that had been felled during the First World War; there were no buildings, no water, no electricity and no gas. There were, however, bread, milk, meat and grocery

deliveries. (Long since discontinued!) It was owned by a semi-
recluse, Mr Teddy Rowe, who lived in a hut at one end of the
property, and he retained this and one acre of land, which we
had the first chance to buy, either on his death or if he wanted
to sell.

This move was going to be much more difficult than the
moving of the hobby farm in 1935. The farm had to keep going
while parts were moved and made ready to take all the stock
and us on one day. We enlisted the help of the 'War Ags', as it
was known; it helped farmers on a hire basis, supplying men,
tractors and trailers etc. The labourers were either too old to be
'called up', conscientious objectors, prisoners of war or land-
girls. We were able to arrange with the labour administrator to
have the same team each day and also ones who were capable
of lifting heavy weights.

It was during the winter months that the move took place,
when the stock of birds was at its lowest level, the fattened
birds having been killed off for Christmas. The completion
date for the land was early February and I was sent with three
small chicken arks and a few rolls of wire netting loaded on my
cart to 'take possession' of the land. During the intervening
time, stock was moved into as few pens and houses and as near
the farm gate as possible. Where possible, netting was taken
down and rolled up, posts pulled up, sheds dismantled and
floors cut along a joist so that they would be easy to rejoin.

In the Vale, in the field which was called Starveacre (and
which you will find on the map of Chesham and District dated
1778) we opened a new entrance, digging off the topsoil and
laying flints to make a road well into the field. There was a very
large stack of flints in the field, as the front twenty yards by
some 350 yards had been dug out for flints for road repairs in
the days before McAdam. A builder by the name of Harry
Aston was found and encouraged out of retirement. His first
job was building dwarf walls and putting in drainpipes with

wooden blocks to receive the floors. The need for dwarf walls arose due to the slope of the field, about one-in-four, with the far end almost on the ground and the front four feet above ground level!

The sheds were loaded on to trailers one at a time and in the order needed to re-erect them. The floors were loaded last, so that they came off first, straight on to the pillars already there to take them and then fixed down. Then the rest of the sections were laid out in their correct position around the floor, the bottom of the sections next to the floor. The first section of the back was bolted to the side section and the whole building was soon reassembled. As we were going to live in one, the builder built breezeblocks within the framework, giving a four-inch thick wall, which was then rendered with sand cement. The ceiling was lined with plasterboard and a sink and an outside loo (Elsan) were put in. A soakaway was dug fourteen feet in depth and five feet in diameter. Chalk was found at four feet, which of course was very good for taking away the washing water. Now we were home and dry and were able to move into our 'new' home. The complete move took just over three months and to achieve this we were working up to sixteen hours a day.

With no water at the farm we made arrangements with Bill Palmer, who farmed at the end of Vale Road about a mile away, to use his hand pump. Water was first pumped into a large bath from which his cattle drank. It was then transferred by bucket to fill our containers carried on my cart, mainly in dustbins with a square of wood floating on top to reduce splashing and loss of water. This was a twice-daily job. We were very pleased when T. T. Boughton of Little Chalfont was able to put a borehole down 100 feet. This was a four-inch bore, with a two-inch rising main pipe, halfway up the hill, so that we would be carrying the water downhill and, as and when we had time to lay water pipes, it would run without help from us. This was the reason for the need to bore so deeply. As the war was still being fought, a lot of the pipes and the pump were second hand. The pump stood six feet tall with a four-foot long handle, which made it easier to lift the water out of the ground. My brother used to pump for two and a half hours while I carried to the pens and filled the water troughs. The next day we would swap around.

It was 1947 before Oppenheimer's of Hatfield made a two-stroke driven reduction box from which a rod connected to the pump handle. This enabled the two of us to carry out the water. This of course saved much time but it was also a hard taskmaster as, unless it was stopped or ran out of fuel, it kept pumping water into the butt and we had to keep going until the watering was done and we could stop the pump! Water for the house was stored in a three foot by two foot by one foot galvanized steel tank, taken each morning to the pump and refilled.

In 1948 the Bucks Water Board sank a borehole half a mile further up the Vale and ran a three weeks' yield test, letting the water run down the side of the road into Chesham. This took the ground water below our pump and we had to add a further eighty feet to the bottom of our bore. This work was again done by T. T. Boughton. Later on, in the early fifties, when electricity was at last brought to the Vale, they fitted a Godwin electrically-driven pump, which pumped the water to a storage tank situated in the wood, at the top of the hill. From here it fed by gravity to all parts of the farm, as and when we were able to afford the piping.

We had to dig by hand a trench thirty inches deep from the pump-house to the storage tank, well over 100 yards, to take two galvanized iron pipes and an underground electrical cable for the control switch. This enabled the unattended working of our water supply. This worked for many years before Boughton's fitted a fully automatic system, complete with pressure pump, to pump the water where it was needed. When the water pressure dropped to twenty pounds, this pump would start and, on reaching forty pounds, would switch off. This still had to have the working head over the top of the bore and the pump at 168 feet down, pumping water into a large storage tank nearby, from which the pressure pump drew its water, pumping into an 'air vessel'.

When all boreholes in the country had to be registered, one of the questions asked was, 'How much water do you use at present?' We hadn't a clue, so father just filled in that the pump was rated at 200 gallons per hour. The licence came back for a yearly abstraction of 1,752,000 gallons. This turned out to be more than was registered by the whole of Devon and Cornwall combined. Later, in the late seventies, when it was very important that there was no loss of supply, due to our processing plant, we had Boughton's sink a further bore, but a six-inch one this time, so that submersible pumps could be fitted. When this was pumping clear, clean, water we took out the old pump and enlarged the bore and fitted a further submersible. These pumps supplied the storage tank, and were run on alternate months. They were still working when we sold the farm. George Harding sank all the boreholes on the farm and I believe our last one was the last he fitted before retiring.

While we erected all the buildings we had from Missenden Road, made new pens and generally got the farm running once more, Harry, the bricklayer, was building our first-ever brick building. No, not a house to live in, but a store where food and fuel for cooking could be kept and the waste from Latimer could be cooked and mixed. The building, about eighteen feet by twelve feet, was made of 'fletton' bricks and had a corrugated iron roof and a five-foot opening, without a door, to allow easy access. This building was still there when we sold up, although it should have been taken down to make it easy for the twenty-five ton lorries that delivered in the seventies to turn.

The mixing was done in an old, three foot by five foot, bacon-salting trough, with the lead lining removed. A wooden malt shovel was used to do the mixing. The food was taken out either in a wheelbarrow or in pails on a yoke, items made in Chesham. With the move over, it was decided that we should concentrate on the laying hens and the turkeys, stopping ducks and rabbits.

Our incubators were housed in a wooden shed and, as supplies of most things were very short, and insulation was not then a first priority, which it should have been, the shed was not insulated. Fluctuating temperature was a big problem when hatching in May and June. As there was no electricity, most of our heating was done with paraffin oil. These incubators had a heat exchanger fitted on one side, with an oil container and a burner with two one-and-a-half-inch wicks. These were set to give the maximum heat required for the coldest part of the day. A damper let out the excess heat from the top of the heat exchanger; an ether capsule, situated just above the tray of eggs, in turn controlled this damper. The hotter it was inside, the more the capsule expanded, lifting the damper higher, thereby allowing the unwanted heat to escape into the room. With the outside temperature in the seventies and the waste heat from the lamps, it was impossible, without opening the incubator doors, to keep the correct temperature of 99.7°F. at the centre of the egg.

Our neighbour had hired a digger to dig a roadway into his property. This was 1946 so it was a pre-war machine, large and clumsy and on tracks, and it dug about four wheelbarrows full at a dig. This was used to dig into the hillside a hole to make a room, with internal measurements of forty-eight feet by twelve feet by seven feet with a six-inch thick reinforced concrete sloping roof. The thinking behind this was that the earth, which was to be heaped over the sides and roof, would insulate the building and give us a room cool enough during the summer to enable turkeys to be hatched with the incubator doors closed, which it did.

The digging out was completed by October 1946. The footing was laid and the wall was up about three feet when the weather closed in. The room had been dug out allowing for a nine-inch fletton brick wall with six-inch reinforced concrete behind. The frost started before Christmas and carried on until March. This meant that no work was done until March, when it was discovered that the frost had brought twelve inches of chalk off the walls. This all had to be removed before building could restart. It also meant much more concrete had to be mixed and there was no ready-mix in those days!

A concrete floor that was sloped to the doorway, for easy washing out each day, completed the building. I will write more about incubation later.

Around this time Mr Gilbert encouraged me to consider keeping bees. One June day one of his hives swarmed. He collected these, put them in a new hive and asked if I would like them. I said that I would ask at home if they would mind me keeping bees and I would let him know the next day. There were no objections and we looked around for a place to put them. When I saw Mr Gilbert and told him that I would give it a try, he said he would close the hive entrance that night and I was to call round with my cart when it got back from the camp. This I did and we made room on the back of the cart to take the hive, which was firmly tied on. There were a few bees buzzing around the entrance, the ones that had spent the night in a flower because it was too dark to get back to the hive. These bees flew all the way following the hive.

On arrival we gingerly carried the hive to its new site and then left it for an hour before opening the door, in case they were a little lively. My mother took me down to Blucher Street to meet a Mr Hobbs who ran the local Beekeepers' Association. He lent me books and told me where I could buy the bees wax sheets that were mounted on wire within a wooden frame. From these the worker bees would build out their combs. This also ensured that the combs, when full, could be lifted out without loss of honey.

A smoker was bought to puff a small amount of smoke into the entrance to make the bees think their hive was on fire. This makes them feed on the honey in case they have to leave in a hurry. It also calms them down and enables the beekeeper to open the hive while the bees are feeding, to see if they need another 'lift' put on, containing new, or better still, empty used honeycombs. If the bees do not have to waste time making wax to build the cells, they only have to repair any damage. The beekeeper is also able to see that all is well and if there is a need to cut out any queen cells to control swarming.

There are three types of cells in a hive. In the lower section are the deeper frames with the worker-producing cells, in which the queen bee lays most of her eggs. Then there are the larger cells, called drones, that are also used to store the honey in. These use less wax and therefore save the workers time, enabling then to collect more nectar. A sheet of metal with slots in allows a worker bee to pass through but neither the queen nor drone (male) bee can. The worker bees will enlarge worker cells to construct both queen or drone cells in the lower part of the hive, when they consider the hive is getting overcrowded. This is the prelude to a swarm issuing from the hive and why the queen cells are removed, ensuring there is a large work-force to gather in the nectar and pollen. When the lifts have most of their cells filled with honey and capped over with wax, it is time to harvest the crop. The complete lift will be removed and replaced with a new set of empty ones. Most of the bees are then brushed gently from the honey-filled frames and the complete lift taken away. To remove the honey, the capping is sliced off the combs, which are then placed into the extractor. Mine could take six frames. Once inside, a handle was turned, spinning the frames round and throwing the honey out. These were then turned around so that other side could be extracted. After standing for two days, while any wax particles floated to the top, the resulting clear honey would be bottled for sale.

I remember collecting a swarm of bees from an apple tree in a neighbour's garden. This was a great mistake! They were wild bees and I ended up with twenty-nine stings and was unconscious for over two hours. I did manage to hive them but they, in time, bred with my other hives and I had to re-queen all of my hives to get rid of that strain, which was very aggressive indeed. Later, when I married and moved 600 yards to the far end of Starve Acre, I moved all of the empty hives to a levelled site near my home and, as there was a swarm, they were placed into these hives. You cannot move a hive full of bees a distance less than four miles to be certain they will not return to their old site. Once I moved a hive only a yard to the left and you could see them flying where the hive had been. They did eventually find the correct place. The full hives of bees that were not a swarm were moved during a cold period during the winter.

CHAPTER 8

My Time in the Royal Air Force

6 FEBRUARY 1946 was the day I had to report to RAF Padgate, where we were kitted out, given a medical and sorted out as to what type of trade we would be trained in. At my interview it was suggested that I should join the RAF Police Regiment, as I was over six feet tall. My reply to that suggestion was 'I only have a few friends now and that that will make sure I make no more. Is there no opening for aero engine mechanics?' As I had been in the Air Training Corps for three years, I am sure this counted a great deal in my being posted to Cosford 2nd School of Technical Training.

After seven days, a train took 120 of us rookies to Sudbury in Suffolk for eight weeks' square bashing. This camp had been established on an ex-American bomber station. Not a thing had been altered; only the bombers had gone. The cookhouse was built for the feeding of 500 men. The only alteration that the British made was to put 1500 men on the camp. The cook-house coped by working three shifts for each meal.

A sergeant, who had served in the Air Force regiment, was in charge of us and he had two 'six-week wonders' to help him. A six-week wonder was a fairly new recruit who (we reckoned) had little brain and was fit only for shouting orders given by others. The first shift was 6.30a.m. You then marched back to your hut, washed and made up your bed. This entailed stripping and folding both sheets and blankets in the correct manner at the foot of the bed, sweeping and polishing your floor space and being on parade by 8a.m. We then had to march down to the airfield about a mile away with full kit and .303

Lee Enfield rifle. The 7a.m. group did ablutions and as much cleaning as they could, then marched down for food and marched back to complete the cleaning of the billet. The 7.30a.m. group had to be ready so that they could go to the airfield from the cookhouse.

One day we were marched about three miles in full kit and rifle to the rifle range where we had to fire five rounds at a target some 200 yards away. We all had to put a penny in a kitty and the best shot was the lucky winner. At the end I was that lucky rookie. There were just over 360 coins to be carried back. Not only was there the weight, but in addition I was not popular with the NAAFI girls when I paid for every thing in pennies! I often wondered if 'lucky' was the right word!

One of our group was an atheist who would not wash himself. One day he was taken and forcibly scrubbed and was quite pink when he returned! When we had church parade, he had to stand to attention at the church door. I did wonder if he was trying to work his ticket!

When we had passed out, we had seven days' leave, after which I had to report to Sutton Coldfield Maintenance Unit. I was there for four weeks and, during that time, I had to help a civilian look after the gardens and pigs. One night I had to go with the detachment that provided the guard for a German Prisoner of War Camp. These worked on the camp during the day. I drew the short straw, as my duty was 2a.m. to 4a.m. I think this time is the hardest time to keep awake. We had fixed bayonets and live ammunition. One day neither the POWs nor the guard were back at their usual time. It was found out later that there had been a camp search, which had revealed many knives that had been stolen from their work place. Were they planning a breakout? I don't know.

In early May, I was posted to Cosford 2nd School of Technical Training. This was a large camp, with facilities to train engine mechanics, airframe riggers, for physical training and for officers' training. There was also a large hospital. The camp was just out side Albrighton, nine miles from Wolverhampton. It even had its very own railway halt.

During the first days, we were assessed, teeth were checked over and any repairs done. From that day I have had my regular check without a miss. Maths had been my best subject at school, so you can imagine my surprise when I failed the test and was sent back to school for a week's refresher. During the first month we had fatigues, which included cleaning the roasting pans at the cookhouse, peeling potatoes, digging out grass from the holes in Sommerfield Track (the track that was used for runways) with bayonets at the officers' training section, sweeping up and general tidying of the camp.

We were only nine miles from Wolverhampton where every Thursday at the Town Hall a dance was held, with a very good dance band. If I remember rightly, it had at least fourteen musicians and was called Ronnie Hancock's Orchestra.

The first three weeks when we started training were spent learning how to file and cut steel and how to scrape the faces of two aluminium blocks so that, when pushed together, they were hard to part. Another test piece was to cut from the centre of a three-inch square by a quarter-inch thick piece of steel, a one-inch square and then, from another piece, cut and file a piece that, no matter which way you tried it, would fit perfectly. One man had been employed by Rolls Royce and was thirty years old. His test pieces looked just like a pencil mark on the metal, so perfect was his work. We also needed to learn all the names of the tools and their uses. We then progressed through the workshop learning about carburettors and magnetos, how to crack test shafts for damage using a magnetic field, oil and iron filings, and how to service Merlin engines from Spitfires and the eighteen-cylinder Hercules, a radial engine with sleeve valves. We were taught how important it was not to wipe one's palm on the crankshaft after it had been degreased ready for rebuilding, as the natural oil from your hand would be sufficient to allow the crankshaft to move out of timing position.

About halfway through the course, we were given five days' leave and I travelled home by train. It was most frustrating to pass through Berkhamsted station and on into Euston and then back out to Chesham, another ninety minutes. I was not feeling very well, which was not surprising as I soon went down with mumps very badly and was unconscious for two days. During that time a telegram came informing me to return to camp at once or the military police would call to collect me. My father sent a doctor's certificate and all was well.

On return to camp I, and five others, were told to go to the airfield and report to a wing commander, who was in charge of the making of a safety film. The main theme was safety on the airfield. A Hillman car was parked on the perimeter track and the aircraft taxiing past hit the car, snapped the wing off and crashed into a building. At least that was the idea. What happened in practice was that the wing hit the car's roof and made a dent but the wing had no damage whatsoever. With the twin engine Oxford back in the hangar, about four feet in from the wing tip the main spar was cut through, as was the underskin.

Next day, another try, and this time the wing just flapped up but returned to look as if nothing had happened. So they abandoned that idea and proceeded to taxi the plane into a concrete building. Before doing so the wing commander had drops of glycerine applied to his face. I did wonder if that was really needed, as I would not have cared too much to taxi into the building. My job in this effort was to enter the aircraft after the pilot had got out and switch the magnetos off. I guess the moral here is an AC2 is not worth as much as a wing commander.

I was allowed to try my hand at taxiing, which is done by revving up the right engine to turn left and vice versa. The tricky part is when to shut down the throttle; this has to be done before you have started to turn. There was no steering wheel, only the throttles. I am afraid it was not a very straight line I kept. This took the best part of the week and meant that I had lost three weeks' training, so our small group were attached to Entry 17 to finish our training. We were learning fast. On the Fatigue Saturday we reported with Entry 17, but just a little away from them, listening to see if our names were called out. They were not, so we just disappeared.

We learned how to service jet engines. When this was complete we had three weeks on airfield practice – how to start engines, firstly with the propeller (no rings on the fingers), then with a winding handle and then with a 'Trolleyack'. This was a petrol-driven generator on a two-wheel trolley, which supplied power to the plane's electrics and enabled the pilot to use the starters, similar to starting a car.

We then sat our exams and I managed to pass as an AC1 Engines. After seven days' leave, some of us had to report back to Cosford where we started an engine-fitter course. This followed much the same pattern as the previous one, but covered the subjects more fully.

At Christmas all of the trainees were given five days' leave, while we fitters were given ten days. I had a Norton ex-dispatch-rider's motorbike that I used to travel home at weekends and on leave. I gave another RAF friend a lift on the pillion. It was 12.30p.m. when we left Cosford and, because of the ice on the roads, we came down the A5. A normal ride home took about three and a half hours. On this occasion we arrived home at 9.50p.m., a journey of nearly ten hours. Extremely cold, we had passed lorries in ditches, had to have our feet on the ground most of the journey but came off only once. After we had thawed out and had a warm drink, I took my friend down to Chesham station where he caught the train to Harrow where he lived.

When we returned to the camp, we found most of the camp closed down and those under training having been sent home again. There was insufficient fuel to keep the training hangars warm. As we had already passed our engineers' exams we were given the job of repairing leaks on the whole camp, but the worst job was guard duty. Once I was guarding the gate to the officers' training college from 8p.m. to 10p.m. in a snowstorm with a bitter northerly wind. We only did a two-hour stretch instead of the usual four hours, because of the cold. This was not the best of places to be given. To make matters even harder, bread was rationed to only two slices per day along with very little heating, anywhere. Times were as hard as the frost.

I came out of the air force on 12 June 1947 on a class 'B' release. The whole hut of thirty-two airmen had just finished our training as engine fitters and were packing our kit bags prior to fourteen days' leave before posting to units across Europe and the near east. I had had my inoculations and was to go to an engine-servicing station in S.E. France. Instead I had to report to the sergeant's office, where I was offered my Class 'B' release to work in agriculture. The date on the papers was 28 February 1947 and this was now early June! There were two of us left in the hut, as one had not received his posting. We had nothing to do for a week but we had learned that if you carried a file of papers, walked with a purpose and saluted officers, nobody would trouble you.

All through the fitter course we had marched to the workshops under our own steam, with one of our own walking alongside as if in charge. Only once were we stopped, by an officer who did not think we were marching smartly. He marched us forward, about turned twice and then sent us on our way. At the weekly games afternoon we would march back to the hut, dismiss and spend the rest of the afternoon in the hut, much better than running about in shorts in the cold. If the truth was known, they did not want the bother.

Then I was sent to Blackpool to be de-mobbed (my demob number was 72) and fitted out with civvies, ration book, clothing coupons and a rail pass, should I have to return. I was only there for one night but I managed to visit the Tower Ballroom and have a dance. It would have been two years before I would have been released, as the Berlin air lift started on 26 June 1948 and lasted until 12 May 1949. Over two and a quarter million tons of cargo were air lifted into Tempelhof Airport during that time. I sometimes wonder what my life would have been had I not taken the early release. I enjoyed my time in the RAF (I still have my uniform) and I learned a lot that has helped me throughout my life.

CHAPTER 9

The Start of the Turkey Industry

THE VERY COLD weather during the 1946/47 winter caused an even more dramatic change in the path our business was to follow. In more normal winters we hatched the chickens from January until the end of March. This year the cockerels were suffering from the cold and were not fertile until the beginning of March, so there had been no chickens hatched by the time the incubators and brooders were required for the turkeys. We did not have enough space to hatch both together. A decision had to be taken that was to alter our way of work and of turkey production within the country. Do we hatch chickens or turkeys? This was the $64,000 question. We could not do both. Father reasoned that, as turkeys were considered to be the most difficult poultry to rear, if we mastered that there should be more money than in rearing chickens. The decision was made in March 1946 that we would change to turkeys only.

The turkeys had a pen partly in front of and partly in the wood, with the only shelter provided by the trees. All the food and water had to be carried in pails on yokes from the bottom of the hill right to the top, twice a day, seven days a week. The eggs were collected five times a day to reduce the loss by crows and magpies. Hurricane lamps were hung on the fence each night to keep the fox away. This, however, did not stop the sudden loss of a bird each day at one period. After keeping watch one night my father found that it was an old badger that was doing the damage. He followed it to its sett, where it was gassed. It was a very costly badger. With no chickens we were able to bring the turkeys down from the wood and utilise the area that the chickens had used. This cut out a lot of the laborious carrying of food and water.

Up to 1948 turkeys had only been produced for the Christmas market and there were none available at other times of the year. At that time there were only four people specialising in turkeys and they were Mrs Smith of Monkton Court, with British Whites, Mr Frank Peel of Norfolk, with Norfolk Blacks, Mr Motley of Middle Wallop and us, both with Bronze turkeys, all producing for the Christmas market. Both Hungary and Eire sent birds to the London markets, as we were not self-supporting.

In 1948, without chickens to rear, we were short of work, especially during January to April. With this in mind I said to my father, **'Do you think turkeys could be encouraged to produce eggs in January as chickens could?'**

'Don't know, boy. Let's try,' was his reply.

From those few words a whole new turkey industry was started.

There was no mains electricity anywhere in the Vale so we had to devise a way of providing light. The old acetylene lamps we used for the chickens were worn out and would not do, so a 1.2-kilowatt petrol-driven generator was purchased from the makers, Arthur Lyon, whose factory was in Chesham. They had relocated from Acton during the war. These were used on motor torpedo boats during the war.

We set about making arrangements to provide fourteen hours of daylight for fifty hens. Dad remembered a saying his grandmother had. 'A male turkey won't be fertile until it has strong sunshine on its back.' This really meant that the male needed thirteen and a half hours of light for three weeks before the female became fully sexually active. Otherwise the hens would lay their first clutch of eggs and they would not be fertile. This would have been a very costly oversight!

By the end of January we had the turkeys producing fertile

Breeding birds in the wood (1946-8).

eggs, which enabled the production of the first poults to be hatched in March. We did not sell any of the first year's early production. It must be remembered that by today's standards we are talking of small turkeys, with the hens about twelve to fifteen pounds and the males twenty to twenty-five pounds. It would be many years before breeding and feeding improvements came into play that gave us the turkeys of today.

However, it did create another problem, as nobody thought of eating turkey except at Christmas. The first of the early birds were ready for killing in September and they had to be sold at a discount. More of how we set about this problem later. The next year, with many more early-hatched hen turkeys available to select our breeders from, we were able to offer early-hatched day-olds. The normal price for a day-old turkey was seven shillings and six pence (37^{1}/2p); we were able to charge ten shillings each (50p). With an extra two months' production we were able to increase our breeding flock quickly to keep up with demand. We had a two-year start on the other breeders and the higher price gave our finances a much-needed boost.

You will recall that my father had constructed a new incubator room in which we had a number of different-sized incubators; these were sold and replaced with new Gloucester, 150-egg (chickens), twin (one above the other) machines. These would take 100 turkey eggs. It required a lot of labour, turning the eggs by hand three times per day. Three times? To make sure that during the longer night period a different side was uppermost. To ensure that all eggs were turned an X was marked on one side and an O on the other. Why turn the eggs? This is to prevent the developing embryo from sticking to the side of the shell and dying. All birds' eggs have to be turned, even wild ones. They do this by gently putting a foot between them and rotating the eggs at the same time. By looking at the empty eggshells you sometimes see outside in your garden, you can ascertain if a baby bird came from it or a magpie or crow has had a feed. If it is clean then it was food, but should the shell be neatly chipped around and you can see the outline of veins on the inside of the shell then there is a new mouth or beak to feed.

It was early days and industry was having great difficulty in getting supplies to make anything. We still had not been able to have electricity brought to the farm and in consequence we had to find an incubator manufacturer who could supply a machine that was heated by oil, with an air-circulating fan that worked off a twenty-four volt generator and storage batteries. We eventually found a firm in Norfolk by the name of Neave who would convert a standard machine for our needs. These held nine trays each side of a heating compartment with a fan to distribute the heat. Each tray held around 100 eggs, depending on egg size, and these trays were placed in the metal rack, which could then be turned to a 45° angle by a handle giving a

The author, on the left, with his father.

full 90° turn at the rear. This enabled us to turn 1,800 eggs in less than a minute, much to my relief! On the twenty-first day they were candled (passed over a light) and all eggs that were infertile, or the chick had died, were removed, before being placed into the Gloucester incubator to hatch, as there was no requirement to turn the eggs during the last week.

Why move to the Gloucester incubators to hatch? A hen chick will pip the shell and be out in four hours. A turkey poult will just pip the shell and then rest for up to twenty-four hours before chipping its way round and hatching. With the Gloucesters, the small area inside meant the air, along with the heat and moisture, could move slowly by convection and did not dry the membrane. We also used a fine-mist garden spray, to spray warm water onto the eggs.

This was very successful and we ordered three more setters from Neave. A setter does not have a hatching part. We had mains electricity connected in 1949 at a cost of £800 just to bring in a three-phase supply. Unfortunately, before they delivered the machines to us, they went into receivership. The receiver, knowing very little about incubation, had fans that had been wired for Scotland, which at that time used 250/270 volts. We did not know this at the time but we soon found out, as the hatches were not all hatching at the same time.

It took many hatches before we found that the eggs from the top were hatching to time but the lower down the eggs had been placed, the later they hatched. We found that there was a variation of two degrees Fahrenheit. We had the fans changed and we went to spreading the week's setting (the name given to eggs placed for hatching) over all the machines instead of using one machine each week – only three trays each side – and moved up each week with the lower tray being the higher the following week. This solved the trouble and we were back to a smooth schedule.

There was considerable work entailed in using the 100-egg Gloucesters, although the much better hatches more than compensated for the cost, but the labour requirement made us look for alternatives. The time that turkeys take to hatch causes a problem in forced-draft machines. The inner membrane will dry out and the poult can stick to the membrane and not be able to turn within the shell. If this is too long, they will die. They can be helped out by pulling the top off the egg and easing them out. This was a regular procedure when the large forced-draft machines came along. (Mr Chalmers Watson, who formed British United Turkeys Ltd. in 1962, baffled Gilbert Harding on *What's My Line* with his mime of removing the egg top.) We tried many makes of forced-draft machines to reduce the labour needed with the small Gloucester machines. The all-in-one, combined setting and hatching Turkeybators, produced by Western Incubators of Hanningfield, had auto-matic turning every hour and their colour coding of the trays

28th day – the chicks have hatched.

ensured excellent incubation. The trays for different weeks' hatching were spread over the whole machine, but they still fell down on the hatching side. Mr Wallace, their chief engineer, spent every hatching day for a season testing different ideas, but could never equal the Gloucesters.

Another big problem was temperature control. We were still using ether capsules to control temperature. These were affected by changes in the weather with the atmospheric lows causing lower and the highs giving higher temperature within the machines. The lows only delayed the hatch while highs caused poor hatching. It was very important that we kept up to date with the weather forecasts to know how to set the controls at night so that we kept an even temperature throughout the whole period of incubation. We even had a barometer in the room to help us guess what was going to happen in the next ten hours. I believe that this helped me to have a good idea as to the weather we could expect. Even today I can read the temperature, wind speed and direction, atmospheric pressure and rainfall from my seat at the computer.

The answer to this problem was the 'contact thermometer', as weather conditions had no effect on their accuracy. These had two wires placed into the mercury column and, when contact was made, a small electrical current would pass to a relay to switch the heat on or off as required. They also helped Mr Wallace to develop the R3 Hatchers. One of the major problems with the all-in-one hatching was firstly the fluff or down that came off the poults as they dried after they had hatched. This was blown around the inside, covering eggs and heaters alike. The other and much more important problem was the heat generated by the poults working to get out of their shells. It was an impossible task as two completely different sets of conditions were required.

To my knowledge the R3 was the first machine in this country to have wet and dry bulbs to control the humidity within the hatchers. Humidity was increased by water sprayed onto the heater coil. Here the humidity was increased during the period the poult had chipped the shell and was resting. The cooling was switched on at 99.9°F. by a solenoid valve opening and allowing cold water from the mains to flow through pipes inside the machine until the temperature had dropped back to 99.7°F. This was needed as the work of chipping around the shell and getting out, coupled with many hatching in a small space, generated a great amount of heat. After this the humidity was dropped back to normal.

The close tolerance required for good hatching was completely unobtainable with the old ether capsules, as they required constant adjustment to compensate for the continual change in barometric pressure, but this had no effect on the contact thermometers. These machines enabled us to dispense with the faithful old Gloucesters we had used for so many years. We did keep one pair and, when we closed down, Derek Kelly had them, along with a number of other turkey memorabilia.

When the poults were hatched, those sold were placed in cardboard boxes in which a nest of hay had been made. The lid could be fitted any of four ways, depending on how warm it would be during their travels. Thirteen were in the bottom box with twelve in the top box, tied together. Most were sent by rail and given a place in the heated guard's van. Two poults per 100 were given to cover any losses during their journey.

A pair of boxes would weigh five pounds and the cost to send them 'all the way' as it was called, was two shillings and four pence (about 12p). The railway had charges for fifty miles, 100 miles, 150 miles and all the way, meaning as far as they went. We dispatched them from Amersham Station as, unlike Chesham, there were no changes on their journey into London, where they just changed to the mainline stations that served the station where they were expected. We had little trouble with this form of transport and they would arrive early the next day. Some people used a box that held fifty poults and had holes in the lid that had only been partly punched out. The trouble with these was that, on a cold day, the boxes could be on a trolley awaiting the train and small children would push the holes out and open more than was needed, and the poults would arrive cold.

Once, I remember, a farmer from the Newbury area ordered 500 poults and arranged for his wife to collect them from our farm. She arrived with three friends, leaving nowhere for the boxes of turkeys to travel! She was apologetic, saying she had thought it was a shame to come with an empty car. I had to drive to Newbury after we had cleaned up and set the eggs. It was 10.30p.m. before I arrived home. As far as I was concerned, she was not the flavour of the month. Today incubators can hold 100,000 eggs, the chicks travel out on conveyer belts and are electronically counted into plastic boxes, which are loaded into lorries that are temperature-controlled and driven as far away as France, Germany and Italy, to the brooding houses that can hold 10,000.

CHAPTER 10

Land

ALL THE TURKEY buildings were erected on our first field, Starveacre, and eventually they covered most of the lower half. Our next purchase was sixteen acres from Mr A. Keen for £800 in February 1948. These two fields adjoined the south-east side of our first field. In 1951 we purchased fifty-five acres from Mr H. R. Moore of Hawridge Court. We would have bought more only they wanted a covenant preventing us from keeping turkeys near their house. It turned out that we never did! The cost this time was £55 per acre. This land had been rented out at ten shillings (50p) per acre and the farmer renting would not pay an increase in rent, saying, 'With all those stones I pay one rent to the landlord and another to the blacksmith' and did not want to buy it.

In December 1954 we bought the remaining acre from the executors of Mr Rowe and in September 1955 we bought four acres from Taylor Bros for £200. They had bought a corner of the fields we purchased from Mr Keen. This was quite a mess, as they had allowed a local timber merchant to dump large butts of trees that had wire and nails and other assorted ironwork buried within. It took three full weeks to burn them up out of the way.

It was not until December 1967 that we were able to buy more land. This time it was land opposite the farm and adjoining the land purchased from Mr Moore. There was a total of 68.25 acres at £139 per acre. The owner of the property in the corner of one of these fields had dug into the hillside right up to the boundary, which gave a six-foot drop, and we considered it dangerous to drive the combine alongside this, considering the steep slope we already had to contend with. We offered three acres to him, which he bought. A further seventeen acres was purchased adjoining the 68.25 acres for the highest sum paid for any of the land – £14,400. Finally eighty-four acres, plus ten acres of woodland, of much better land than any of our other land, were bought at £405 an acre. This land was behind the wood and was reasonably level.

We built a small bungalow in 1947 so that we could move out of the converted hen-house. Being so soon after the war, the size was restricted to 960 square feet. There were two bedrooms, a bathroom, kitchen, dining-room and lounge. Father and mother had one bedroom while my brother and I shared the other. There was one definite disadvantage in living with mother. She had the annoying habit of rearranging the furniture, without warning. Your bed could be in one place when you went out at night and rearranged when you got back. With no electricity, moving about in the dark was a real hazardous situation! This bungalow was occupied by my mother until her death in 1989, with no alterations. In 1951 we built a house for me, at the far end of the field so that the turkeys were housed between the two of us. It was completed while we were on our honeymoon. On our return we found the house finished, and the furniture piled up in the centre of the respective rooms. So we had to set to and assemble the bed before we could retire.

As turkey production increased so did the need for more staff, so two cottages were added. Finally, another bungalow was built for my son David, and later occupied by my daughter Margaret and son-in-law Henry. With both the bungalows and my house, we were the builders, in that we employed good tradesmen to do the work while we purchased all materials, making sure that we bought good materials with good discounts. I also worked in any spare time as 'the Boy' and, learned a great deal from the tradesmen on how to, why, and the need to be always ready to help. They were pleased to teach me. This stood me in very good stead, as were able to do all the groundwork for steel-framed buildings, which was how most of our turkey houses were constructed. We even made from scratch one building 168 feet by sixteen feet We had a quote for a building 420 feet by thirty-two feet, which we thought was too dear and, on querying how they came to such a price, we were told that the high cost was mainly for digging and concreting the holes for the erection of the uprights. We bought a digger to fit on the back of one of our tractors, marked out the upright positions, dug the holes and put in concrete level rods. When this was ready, but before concreting, the levels were checked by one of their staff. He passed fourteen of the levels but had us knock down by half an inch the level rods in twelve others. Before the erectors started, I pointed out that we had been told to lower the said concrete, and much to my joy they had to place half-inch thick metal plates in these holes to bring the levels up.

Men and horses provided the power on the farm when I first started. Among one of the most arduous jobs in those early days was 'mucking-out' or cleaning the yards and buildings where the animals had been wintered. My introduction to this was when I helped clean out buildings while waiting for my pony and cart to return from the camp. Cattle used to come in from the fields November/December time and not go out again until the grass started to grow, about April. Their sheds and yards would be bedded down with wheat straw and the cattle fed on barley and oat straw, plus hay and roots and maybe ground oats. Then the straw was long and undamaged compared with the straw from today's short straw varieties that has been broken up by the combine harvester and cut by the baler in the baling process.

It was a really hard job, pulling forkful after forkful from the floor and pitching towards the doorway, if the cart could not enter the building. Here another person would then pitch it into the cart. The carter would take his loaded cart to the field in which the root crop was to be grown the next year. Here he would back the cart up to the heap being made at the edge of the field. Some carts then had to be emptied by hand, but if the cart was of the type that would tip, he would remove the tail board and take out a pin; the cart would tip and the carter would move his horse forward to complete the emptying. Sometimes a hay knife was used to cut the manure into squares to make it easier to remove. In the yards you just pitch straight into the cart. I remember a local farmer had employed the 'War Ags.' labour gang to clean one of his yards. After working for just over a week, the foreman reported that they had finished. He was asked if he had found a yard of chain. The answer to this was no, so he was told to 'carry on until you find it.' They took another ten days before the chain was found!

Come the autumn, after harvest the heap from the edge of the field had to be reloaded on to the carts and taken to make small heaps across the field. The back-board would be removed and, with a long-handled drag fork, the manure would be dragged off the cart into small heaps at twice the distance a man could spread while standing by the heap. When this was completed it was spread evenly across the field by hand fork. Any lumps had to be shaken out. This would have taken three carts and five or six men four or five weeks to complete, depending on how many cattle had been wintered.

Compare this to to-day's method, when a tractor with a loading fork on the front is used to do the loading of the trailers, which will carry ten tons, as will the manure spreaders. Before the equipment was so big, we did our own cleaning out and spreading with our own equipment. But our size and the cost later on made us use contractors. They could fill one of our six-ton trailers with six fork loads. With two tractors and trailers and one man of our own, and the contractor and loader, the work was done in less than half the time it would have taken us. To spread the manure, a contractor would arrive with three tractors plus spreaders, and a loading tractor and three men. The third tractor and spreader would be loaded while one would be spreading and one travelling.

Now this had to be ploughed in. Depending on the type of farmland one had, it would be one-, two- or three-horse land. This indicated how many horses were needed to pull a plough. The horseman was one of the higher paid of the work force but he worked longer hours. He would start between 5.30 and 6 o'clock in the morning, when he would feed and groom his horse or horses. He would then fill the nosebags with feed for the midday break and put on the saddle, collar, aims and bridle. The aims fitted around the collar, which had been put over the horse's head, but upside down. Once it was on the top part of the neck, it would be turned the correct way up. It fitted just down on the chest and it was from here that all the pulling was done via the aims and traces. The saddle supported the traces or the shafts. Next the bridle would be fitted, by placing the bit, a bar of metal, which could be straight or pivoted in the middle and with rings on either side. Then the top would go over the ears and fasten down the side of the head. Now, according to the work for the day, the correct length reins would be connected to the rings on the bit. For ploughing they would be plough lines, which were like sash cord and much longer than the reins used when pulling a cart. Had we been carting, breeching and crupper would have to be fitted. This is the braking system to prevent the cart running over the horse and it is also used to back the cart. The crupper went under the horse's tail and a strap went from there to the rear of the saddle to prevent its movement forward. It also supported the breeching, a thick, wide strap that was connected to a hook on either side of the shafts, with similar hooks in front to take the traces from the collar. In this way horsepower was applied to move things around.

At 7a.m. they would be ready to move to the job in hand. When we were working in the field, we would not be near the stables until the work was finished or it was knocking-off time. On two-horse land the ploughman would ride on the first horse, while leading the second, which would carry the two nosebags and a few ploughshares. When he arrived at the field, the nosebags would be placed in the hedge, along with the ploughman's breakfast and lunch and the ploughshares. As the horses worked side by side pulling the plough, there would be a double whippletree on to which the traces would fit. There would only be one set of plough lines (reins) and the bit rings in the centre would be connected by a short strap. A good pair of plough horses could work all day without need of much guidance from the ploughman. The plough would have a pair of metal wheels at the front, then the plough. The share would cut into the soil with the mouldboard behind to invert the soil. To keep a straight side to the furrow, a blade (coulter) was fixed to make a vertical cut near to the share. The width of soil turned over would be six to eight inches at a time and it would be four to six inches deep.

The field would have a furrow ploughed around it, following its shape. Then, starting from one side, the ploughman would mark out the lands. The first one would be eleven yards in from the headland, while the rest would be twenty-two yards. The ploughman would then proceed to plough the 'opening' furrow. Starting at his eleven-yard mark, he would pull a shallow furrow towards his eleven-yard marker on the opposite headland. He would then turn round and plough another, making a sixteen-inch wide ploughed area. Again he would turn and this time plough this to full depth, turning his first furrow back where it had been, with the third furrow covering the first, turning and repeating this on his second furrow. This ensured that all the ground would be ploughed. The skill comes in making these two furrows just meet and not overlap. He would mark out two or three 'lands' before starting to plough the field by ploughing down one side of the first opening and up the second opening. This is called 'casting'. This is continued until there are only eleven yards still to be ploughed. The plough then comes up the other side of the first opening and continues 'gathering', until the other ploughed land is reached, when the last furrow is ploughed less deep. This continues until the field is ploughed. Finally, the 'headland' where the horse and plough turned is ploughed by going round and round. A considerable amount of walking is needed to plough just one acre.

T.T. Boughton had two steam engines that had very large cable drums attached horizontally underneath them. These pulled an eight-furrow plough across the field. A man rode on this to steer. On reaching the other side, he would lift the plough out of the ground and lower the other set of bodies that would plough the soil the same way. This was called a one-way plough. The drivers of the steam engines would talk to one another by means of the steam whistles, so that they knew when it was their turn to start pulling the plough towards them.

Compare that to to-day's tractors with horse-power from thirty-five to 300, pulling one-way ploughs with four to twenty furrows, ploughing with up to a fourteen-inch wide furrow ten inches deep with only one man and no marking out. In addition electricity does all the hard work in the buildings. Though they still work long hours when the weather is right, the word 'hard' has been taken out.

Being close to London we were handy for photo calls around Christmas, when the press wanted photos of turkeys. We would have a phone call enquiring if they could bring a star, starlet, or pin-up down. We had many, including Yana and

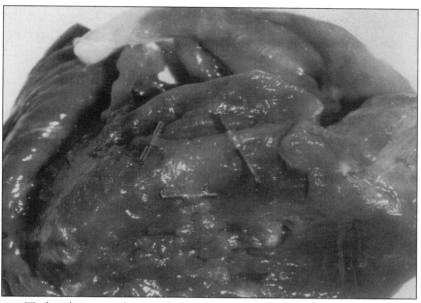

Turkey heart used in medical research at Charing Cross Hospital Medical School. The nerve is shown going over the pins.

Vivian Blain. The hospitals would send students to harvest eyeballs from turkey heads, after they had been removed in the evisceration process. These were then used for dissection in their training at Moorefields Eye Hospital. The Oxford Blood Bank would come and collect about three or four gallons of fresh blood on slaughter days and this was used during tests on human blood. A doctor from Charing Cross Hospital Medical School needed to find the nerve that worked the top and bottom vessels of the heart. For this we provided hearts removed directly the bird had been killed. Some of this work led to the heart by-pass operations of today.

CHAPTER 11

Feeding Turkeys

MY FATHER started to formulate our turkey feed during the war and the mixture of things that were cooked to supplement the bought-in feed was very diverse. Not much work had been done on turkey nutrition before the war and it was quite a while after it ended before real headway was made. He bought Ewing's book on poultry nutrition from the USA as well as the *Feed Bag Red Book*, a monthly compounders' magazine giving tables of ingredients with their vitamin, mineral, energy, protein etc. content.

In the early days before the old breeds had been genetically improved and before it was possible to buy the many ingredients that go into to-day's highly efficient rations, one found great difficulty in making balanced feeds. At one time we were buying food from Levers, and we were getting white barring in the wing feathers, due to a low lysine content in the ration. Around this time we found BOCM literature inside the Lever feed bags. Unilever had BOCM supplying feed direct from the mill. Levers supplied feed sold by local reps in direct competition with each other. A very well-kept trading secret was out.

During the war and for a number of years afterwards, it was a case of making the best of a bad job. We were very fortunate in having a supply of fish heads etc. from the local fish shop. Fish meal has always been a very good source of protein, or more correctly of amino acids, though too high an inclusion can impart to the meat or eggs a fishy tang.

As the supply of feed became easier to buy, we had a three-phase supply of electricity connected to the farm at a cost of £800 in 1949. This, without doubt, enabled us to move forward more rapidly. We installed a half-ton Adelphi horizontal mixer at a cost of £300. This we were told would mix the ingredients in three minutes from the time everything was in the mixer. Later Bob Pauling of Vitamealo found it required four minutes, when he took samples from five bags as they came off the mixer, i.e. every other bag. Their concentrate contained a tracer element, which should have been at the same level in all samples. This was not achieved until mixed for four minutes.

When in 1991 we needed a replacement spur gear for the mixer, I rang the factory, and the person who answered the phone remembered our order and the particular mixer. I thought this was most impressive. This was the only replacement we needed in fifty years. Not even the belts were ever replaced.

A three horsepower Christy Norris hammer mill did all the grinding, blowing the ground wheat and maize into separate holding bins. The barley and oats were always ground together, one part oats to two parts barley, blown into a third bin. We have always used oats in all of our rations, in spite of the fact that oats have always been looked down on, as they are relatively low in energy and high in fibre, compared to maize, wheat and barley. Nevertheless, the inclusion of oats in any ration gives a better finish i.e. whiter fat. The fibre helps to prevent feather picking (pulling and eating feathers off other birds in the pen), and litter eating. Birds, just like humans, need fibre to help the digestive system move things along and to make the best of the ration. I believe oat husk is better than litter eating, and feather eating is not to be encouraged.

One Saturday afternoon in November, on one of my father's weekends off, he was entertaining a Mr Eves, I believe, who had come down to discuss the making of a vitamin A and D3 supplement. At that time no one was manufacturing any vitamin or mineral supplements. We were using alfalfa meal, and grass meal when alfalfa was not available, to supply A and D3, but it was a variable quantity at that time. From that meeting a supplement was developed based on irradiated grass meal that could be added to the ration giving a known amount of vitamin A and D3. This eventually led to a whole new industry developing to supply vitamins and minerals etc. to the feed industry.

At one time we were using dried brewers yeast very success-fully until, unbeknown to us, they started to extract riboflavin to make into tablets to sell in the chemists' shops. The by-product was then sold to the feed industry. We did not find this out until the birds started to show signs of a deficiency. We were fortunate to obtain a large number of tins of concentrated yeast that had been made to improve the health of people in the West Indies, but which they would not use. Most likely it had been taken from the extracted yeast we had been sold.

We were not so fortunate in the 1980s with a firm that was making for us a protein concentrate that only required the addition of soya bean meal and cereals. We were buying starter crumbs to feed the young turkeys for the first six weeks, then they were fed on our own produced feed for the rest of their lives. Because we did not feed any drugs or growth promoters, they had to have a special vitamin and mineral supplement mixed for us and they had to buy three months' supply at a time. We started to lose turkeys from twelve weeks old onwards. Six weeks is the time taken to use up any stored vitamin A. They would just keel over, flap their wings and die. The Ministry closed us down for a week until they had proved that it was not fowl pest. After weeks of worry and greater losses, a Ministry veterinarian at Reading thought that it could be vitamin A deficiency. He took a sample of the protein concentrate, and on analysis he was proved right. This was confirmed when the supplement was also analysed. The cost to

The author with Bob Pauling.

us was £48,000, which was paid to us in compensation, though it was in no way able to compensate us for all the stress and worry we had had.

In the early days of mixing feed, the only way we had to move the sacks, which weighed at least one hundredweight (fifty kilograms), was by a sack barrow or carried on your back. To raise a sack to the required level, you needed to get it on to your back, by using a sack-hoist, which was a platform. As you turned the handle, two chains wound around a drum raising the platform and sack. If there were two of you, you would stand either side of the sack facing the way you wanted to go. You gripped your mate's hand behind the sack and with the other hand pushed the corner of the bottom of the sack in to make a hand pocket; then you just lifted!

We had to raise all these up to the first floor, and for this we used a chain-operated hoist. A sack would have a small chain made for the job, in that you placed the chain around the neck of the sack. One end would thread through the other end and then it would be placed on the hook of the hoist. Once up, it would be wheeled to a hopper that fed the hammer-mill below, which held about a ton of grain when filled level. All the sacks had to be manhandled into the hopper and this required two men with strong backs. One can hardly wonder that I slipped a disc three times. But three days on a hard board seemed to do the trick for me, I'm pleased to say.

The meal, when ground, was blown by the mill into one of three bins, from which it had to be shovelled into one-hundredweight sacks, and once more hauled up to the first floor! There it was then tipped into the ten-hundredweight mixer along with the other ingredients. After the mix was ready, it was sacked off into the sacks that the fishmeal was delivered in; then, if it was not fed straight away, a coloured string was used to secure the open top. The colour was the means of coding as to the age of the birds it was to be fed to. This worked very well and was used until we closed down. We did have a very big scare, when one day an employee came to me with an electric cable to which he was fixing a plug top and asked me which were the red, blue and green wires. When asked how he knew which sack had which colour string tying it up, his reply was 'I remembered the order that the sacks were stored.' Luckily we did usually store in the same place, but not always. To prevent any further problem happening again, we also placed a card with the colour written on it, on the sacks of feed.

Over the years improvements were made to the way we had to handle the ingredients. The first to be replaced was the two-hundredweight chain hoist, with an electric ten-hundredweight one, which also travelled on a RSJ. This enabled six sacks of meal to be raised and pulled over to rest safely on the upper floor. Then with the coming of the combine and bulk storage of cereals, grain driers and conveyors, we erected a seventy-ton grain store of five bins in a 'u', with an auger in the middle. This auger was also used to fill the hopper above the hammer mill, after being re-sited and an additional seven and a half horsepower mill added. This made life a lot easier. They still blew the meal into bins that required it to be bagged and weighed but we raised the floors and sloped them to enable a sack to be filled by just lifting a sliding door. We still had to weigh and take them to the first floor to be put into the mixer.

These were later replaced with self-emptying hoppers with metering augers in the bottom; these would empty one hundredweight per minute. The barley/oats mixture was weighed by a trip-scale, as we could not be certain that the mix was always the same. We replaced the trailer and sacks with a feed-wagon, which was filled by an auger fitted under the mixer and carried two half-tons, and, the hoppers were filled without the driver getting off the tractor seat. This was a great time saver and it enabled one man to mix and feed seventy tons a week without strain.

The actual task of formulating a ration took my father three days per ration with pencil and paper. With the advent of calculators, we were able to reduce this to a day. Some times when using the calculator, which cost £350, we would find a totally incorrect figure on the display. It took weeks to find the cause. The office was on the same supply as the cold store and when the compressor motors switched on, causing a momentary drop in voltage, this was enough to lose the calculation. The first calculators did not have a printout!

Around 1977/78 there was a food ration computer on sale for around £5,000. I could not bring myself to spend that amount of money on a one-application machine. We were pleased we didn't, as very soon afterwards Commodore Computers launched their 'Pet Computer.' I went to the local shop which was selling them, and which was run by a friend of mine, to have a look at what was on offer. The first ones had a very small keyboard which, with my rather large hands, I thought it would be difficult to operate. I was told that he was expecting the first typewriter-type keyboard to be delivered during the next week. This would have a massive 16K of memory and a tape recorder to save one's work on. Disk drives and printers would not be available until early in the next year. The cost would be £695. This was in May. I went home and discussed with Brenda, Margaret and Henry if we could afford to purchase this. In the end we did buy it and I had to learn how to use it. There was nobody one could turn to for help and I had to make do with the few books that were available. It was the end of July before I had written a programme that allowed me to enter the weight of the different ingredients and it would do the calculations for me. I would try a mix, copy this off the screen and then try another, repeating this until I achieved a ration that was the cheapest that would do the job. At that time we were using starter crumb mixed by our protein concentrate supplier, followed by four further rations we mixed ourselves. To give an indication of the amount of food eaten by 100 turkeys, in the first week they will have eaten nine kilos, at ten weeks old 520 kilos, at twenty weeks old 2,100 kilos and by twenty-six weeks old 3,765kg. There was saving of £150 per week on our food bill by August!

In January the next year we were able to buy both a dual floppy disk drive, using five inch disks, and a printer. It took a lot of midnight oil before I could format the columns of figures on the printer. The instruction to programme the formatting code was '.9999.999'. However, it should have placed four numbers before the decimal place, and three after it. This wasted hours of time, and I was working on this after a full day's work on the farm. In desperation, I tried '9999.999' dropping the point at the start. It worked perfectly. I could willingly have wrung the proof-reader's neck.

Vitamealo concentrate being added to the mixing machine.

As we used a concentrate to supply the vitamins, minerals and some of the protein needed, we only needed to use wheat, barley/oats, soya meal, meat and bone meal (until BSE stopped its use), limestone flour and di-calcium phosphate to make a balanced ration. We had to calculate amounts supplied by each ingredient, the most important of which were protein, energy, lysine, fibre, calcium, phosphorus and salt, and then the price. Even in this simplified form you can see that rations made up of only seven ingredients required looking up eight values for each or a total of fifty-six searches and calculations to arrive at the values that this mix would give.

It is obvious why one ration took my father three days' work, and he might still not end up with the most cash-effective mix. With both the disk unit and a printer, life became much easier to work out rations. I remembered that David Filmer, a nutritionist, had given a talk on the way turkeys were being fed

Feeding fattening birds, 1951.

too little protein during the first part of an eight-week period and too much in the last four weeks. In those days most people were using a starter, a grower and a finisher ration; indeed, some still do. To counter this we made our changes every three weeks for the females and four weeks for the males, the males being fed a week longer as they were growing more rapidly than the females and needed more protein. Years later I met David again and told him what we were doing and why. He was most interested and later he marketed a unit that would add wheat to the broiler feed as the birds grew. Whether this was as a result of our talk or because he was already working on those lines, I do not know.

Since the early days of computers I have always been very interested in them. I went on to write many programmes for our own use in costing etc. I even wrote a wage programme that I sold locally. It would work out holiday entitlement, bonus pay, even including the number of coins and notes needed. One day in 1994 I received a phone call from one of the users. His computer had broken down. Would I please write a wage programme for his new computer? I declined his request, as these could be bought from any computer shop. At one computer show I was stopped by two Norwegian lads who were looking for someone to market their spreadsheet. Unfortunately, I could not make use of their offer. Another time I was offered a partnership with a friend importing and marketing coloured disks for the three and a half-inch drives. He had obtained a franchise to import them but did not have enough capital.

CHAPTER 12

Rearing Turkeys

EARLY IN THE BOOK I wrote about rearing with broody hens. With the extra birds we were now rearing, we required a less labour-intensive system. Mr Motley, of Middle Wallop, near Andover, who was a much larger producer than us, had designed a brooder heated by a paraffin lamp with a twenty-four inch square flat top with curtains around the sides to retain the heat. He also floated the Andover Timber Company to market them and other turkey-rearing equipment. These were very successful, each brooder rearing forty poults to eight weeks. Later we fitted an outside run to give more room. At eight weeks old the birds were moved to their rearing/fattening quarters. These were pens made from steel angle bolted together with a four-inch by one and a quarter inch timber frame on which two-inch chain-link netting four feet wide formed the floors; they were about two and a half feet off the ground. Two inches of concrete made a place for the droppings to rest to enable them to be cleaned up more easily. This was partially a mistake, as heavy prolonged rain would wash the droppings into the walkway. We had to keep the turkeys off the ground, otherwise blackhead (a disease of the liver) would kill at least half of the birds before they were ready for the table.

During 1947 while I was in the RAF, the Ministry of Agriculture had conducted experiments with different drugs to combat this scourge on our farm. They had found an arsenical drug that could be injected into the thigh muscle. This did save the birds but was very time-consuming. Drugs like Turkey-San came onto the market. These could be added to the drinking

Motley brooders.

water but not into automatic drinkers, as the drug was diluted as they drank, thus reducing its effectiveness. The best drug, marketed by May & Baker, was named Entramin. We were able to discontinue using this drug in the 1980s and we had no further trouble.

Food was still rationed and we grew lucerne for spring and summer and kale and fodder beet for the autumn. The lucerne and kale were cut by hand daily and fed in racks to prevent the turkeys walking all over and spoiling much of it. The beet was shredded and mixed raw with their feed twice a day. Cutting kale by hand and loading could be a wet, cold and very miserable job and it then had to be handled again into the racks. To further help to rear more turkeys without incurring high capital expense, we developed a hay box. Firstly, we made frames that could be placed at the shelter end of the fattening pens. These had wire netting on both sides and the space

Motley brooders with extensions.

between was filled with hay. On the top was a sack also filled with hay. This enabled the birds to be moved from the Motley brooder at four weeks thereby doubling the throughput. These frames were removed when the birds were six to eight weeks old, depending on the weather. The warmer the weather, the sooner the hay boxes could be removed and used for the next lot of youngsters.

This system was very labour-intensive and there was a need to rear birds off the wire mesh floor, as the improvement in weight gain, due to selection and improvement in the rations for the birds, was causing breast blisters. Birds with breast blisters were downgraded and had to be sold at a discount. This made our search for a better method very urgent. We reasoned that if we covered the pen floor with clean straw it should stop the turkeys picking up the caecum worm that carried the blackhead protozoa; this was tried out with the first early-

Hay box.

hatched birds from the lighting trials. It was partly a success, with only a few contracting blackhead. These were removed as soon as they were seen. This, however, did not reduce the chore of filling forty-eight oil lamps every other day.

About this time the Labour Government's ill-fated Gambia egg scheme collapsed. Much of the unused brooding equipment was bought by Cope & Cope, of Reading, from whom we purchased two Jamesway (American) four-tier brooders, (later increased to four) but with only a 200-watt heater per tier. These had to be housed in a room heated to 70°F. We used an oil-fired Agamatic boiler. We purchased a shed forty feet long, twelve feet wide and seven feet to the ceiling to house these. The timber came from old telegraph poles, and was insulated with glass wool. We removed the earth from the top of the incubator room, and laid a levelling concrete floor on which to erect this building, leaving an eight-foot area clear before the door. The poults came direct from the incubators below on a Tuesday and into the Jamesway brooders where they had food, water, warmth and light. The first night the lights were turned off; the next two nights they had light for twenty-four hours. This was reduced to normal daylight before they were moved on the following Monday. This building with the brooders was highly successful and was still used to start the last turkeys we produced.

On the area that was used by eight homemade brooders and reared 320 birds at a time, we erected nine thirty-feet by eighteen-feet, half-round asbestos sheet buildings. They required three sheets to make a half-round section. These were placed on nine-inch wide dwarf brick walls on which was placed a pre-cast concrete block, which was long enough to take one sheet, and in the top was a channel about three inches deep and three inches wide. The sheets were placed into this, one each side, and then lent onto a specially-made wooden frame that was moved along as the building progressed. A third sheet completed the half-circle and was held in place with twelve bolts. Two holes were cut into the roof to allow light in and covered with Perspex sheet. Ends with doors and windows were made from two-inch by two-inch framework and clad with shiplap timber.

The interior was lined with aluminium foil (at that time a very new insulating material), then covered with eight-foot by four-foot sheets of flexible asbestos. Water, electricity and fans for ventilation were added. We were advised by Vent-Axia that one six-inch and one nine-inch fan with three speed controllers would be more than adequate for four hundred turkeys to eight weeks old. It must be remembered that a lot of the work reported in this book was at the forefront of its time. The ventilating capacity of these two fans was not enough. We found, by trial and error, that two twelve-inch fans would just do the job. The brooders were also home-made from two six-

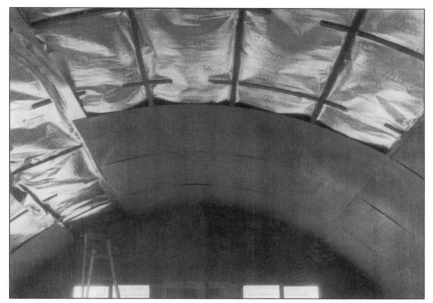

Aluminium sheet insulation.

foot by thirty-inch flat sheets of galvanized steel, nailed to two-inch by one-inch timber frame, the space being packed with glass fibre insulation. Legs were set at an angle, with six inches of galvanised sheet making a skirt around the top to keep the heat in. Six 200-watt Myclax heating panels, controlled by a Western Thermostat, provided the heat. The floor was covered with hardwood shavings from a local woodenware factory. Food troughs were made from the six-foot by thirty-inch sheets of galvanised steel thirty inches long, three inches wide and one and a half inches high. The height and size were increased as the poults grew. As these took over from the Motley brooders, we put up two more half-round sheds but this time they were sixty-six feet long and we could rear 1,000 poults on the floor. This was considered a lot of turkeys to have in one group at that time. Nowadays 10,000 would be nearer the number. The biggest problem with these sheds was that we

Home-made brooder and food trough.

were on a slope and slowly getting tight on space. We could only clean out the litter from one end and at that time there were no small mechanical loaders available, so it was shovels and wheelbarrows, though even this was a great saving over the labour requirements of the Motley brooders.

By this time all birds were being reared in straw yards very successfully, but only part of the pens had cover. Although life for both the birds and for us who looked after them was very much better than rearing in the open fields, which we tried when the blackhead drugs were available, we vowed to replace all the rearing/fattening pens with covered, wind-protected ones, as much for the birds' comfort as for our own. We hear a lot about free-range rearing. This is lovely on fine warm days, but how many weeks can we rely on it to be like that? Having reared turkeys on free range and in open-fronted buildings with fresh air and sun, I know which the birds, and those who look after them, prefer. Not standing about in rain and mud, thank you very much.

For us, we found that pens sixty feet long by twenty feet wide were ideal, as we had the feeding troughs along the front only. If we made the pens wider, they would hold more birds than there was space for the required number of feeders, bearing in mind the slope of the field. We could only service one side as the other was either up in the air or built into the hillside. When building new pens we had to dig into the hillside and, with the soil, build up the lower side. We would aim at a building 180 feet long and twenty feet wide (three pens each holding 200 birds), with a fifteen-foot roadway and a further building opposite, both facing towards the centre. The ends and back were sheeted in but the front left open. The feed hoppers provided protection up to four feet and for really bad weather we could unroll windbreak sheeting.

By the late 1960s we needed more space to rear the turkeys, so we removed the nine half-round asbestos sheds and replaced them with one building 120 feet by sixty feet, made of wood, fully insulated and power ventilated, with automatic feeding and Calor gas-heated brooders. We only removed the soil to thirty-five feet from the roadway, and then a nine-inch brick wall was erected down the centre of the plot. The top far corner was six inches below ground level, while the front corner diagonal was eleven feet above ground level. With five divisions inside we could rear 1,000 per week to six weeks – one week in the tier brooders, five weeks in this house, leaving one week to clean, disinfect, and blow in the chopped wheat straw for litter. We had to be very particular when baling the straw from behind the combine, making sure no straw that was damp was baled. We would even turn it to be certain it was dry. Mould would quickly kill the poults with aspergillosis, a fungal disease of the respiratory tract.

At six weeks old the poults were moved to the straw yards where they stayed until they were of the weight required for killing. The pens were only cleaned out once per year. All the manure was taken to one of the fields on which we grew corn. Here it was clamped until after harvest when it would be spread. When we took over fields from other farmers, they were usually low in all nutrients. After ten years, the fields were so high in phosphate and potash that we needed very little artificial fertilizer or bag muck, as it has been called. On the better land three and a half tons of wheat was normal. When we first started growing corn one and a quarter tons was considered a very good crop. I think this needs a little explanation. Whilst the yields have been pushed up by greater knowledge and higher yielding seed, it has to be remembered that with the combine harvester the corn is cut and threshed in the field, as opposed to the following operations before the general use of combines, all of which caused loss of grain. The grain was cut and tied into a sheaf and thrown by the binder on to the ground, then picked up and placed in stooks to ripen. Here birds could partake of a feed as and when they wished. If the weather should be wet then the grain would germinate, which meant another loss. In a dry year it took about ten days to be dry enough to cart and stack. There was an old saying that if the crop was oats, it had to hear the church bells three times between cutting and carting. As we did not work on a Sunday at corn cart, this then meant at least sixteen days before it was pitched on to a cart/trailer where it had to be built correctly to enable it to travel to the rick yard. The loader had to walk on the sheaves knocking more grain loose. Now if it was not to be threshed, and rarely was this the case, a rick had to be built, which meant more throwing about and more walking on. If the rick had been poorly built or thatched, rain would get in and spoil more. The grain now became a very good supply of food for rats and mice, and the longer it waited for threshing the more they ate.

Only one more operation was now left to do – threshing. This required pitching the sheaf from the rick onto the top of the machine where the band cutter cut the string that had been tied round the sheaf when it was first cut. How much grain had been lost? I do not know for sure, but quite a lot I think. It is worth mentioning the workings of this last operation. There would be two or three men on the rick, the band cutter steadily feeding the cut sheaves into the drum. The band was carefully kept and used to tie the full sacks of corn. There would be one man 'on the corn'. He would be responsible for weighing the filled sacks, tying the mouths of the sacks and carrying and stacking the sacks, which, if it were wheat, would weigh two and a quarter hundredweights. As if that were not enough, he had to remove the full sacks from the machine and replace them with empty ones. On odd occasions there could be three needing to be removed at the same time. This was my job in the team.

The dustiest job of all was the removal of the chaff from underneath the machine. Then if the threshed straw was to be baled, you needed a man on either side of the baler, one to put the needle in to enable the two wires to be pushed through and then back again where they were threaded through a pre-formed loop and twisted together. These bales weighed three quarters of a hundredweight and had to be carried away and stacked in a rick. When you came to the last three feet or so, this is where the fun began. The law required that the rick be encircled with a roll of wire netting, a minimum height of two feet, to prevent the rats escaping. Dogs would have been

Free-range turkeys in the 1950s.

waiting for this time to arrive. As the rick got lower, so the rats would start to run. There could be as many as 100 if the farm cats had been fed too much. You may have seen workers with their trouser legs tied with string, just below the knee. This is to prevent rats running up inside the trouser leg. Many a rat has tried to escape that way and I have even had a mouse running across my shoulders under my shirt. Today, one man in a combine has no problem in harvesting 100 acres per day, with two men carting the grain and one more looking after the drying, cleaning and storing. If the crop were a good one, then there would be up to 400 tons of grain, all harvested, moved and stored by simply pulling leavers and pressing buttons.

When we were producing heavy weight stags (thirty to forty pounds eviscerated) from late April to early September, we found that the fat, which lined the underside of the skin, over the crop area, would change from a creamy colour to a watery grey and had to be removed. As well as taking time there was a loss of nearly three-quarters of a kilo. We were able to prevent this happening by keeping them in light-controlled houses from sixteen weeks until killing. It occurred as the birds started to become sexually active. By restricting them to eight hours of light, we were able to prevent this development. We also found that it was October before turkeys would put on a layer of fat normally. However, experiments at the MAFF experimental husbandry at Gleadthorpe in the early Eighties found that 15°C. was the most profitable temperature to rear heavyweight turkeys. It was also found that at 21°C. the food conversion ratio was at its best but, along with a considerable feed saving, there was a loss in body weight. Each unit of body weight lost was worth four times as much as the equivalent unit of food saved. Likewise, a fall below 15°C. caused an increase in feed consumption without a corresponding weight increase. These experiments were instigated by Jim Binstead of ADAS after a visit to our farm, when we were discussing how to achieve all-the-year-round production of turkeys with the natural finish that was attainable on birds produced for the Christmas market. Jim was attached to the Ministry at Wolverhampton and the work was reported in *Poultry World* (29/01/1981).

We found that our covered straw yards gave us a quality bird that still retained the flavour that our customers demanded. The birds had sunlight, fresh air, and room to run around and flap their wings. They cost more to produce but were always in demand. The supermarkets' relentless pursuit of cheaper and yet cheaper produce has been responsible for the demise of the smaller butcher shops, which in turn has led to the loss of many smaller turkey producers due to their continual use of the turkey as a loss leader at Christmas, sometimes at a retail price 50 per cent lower than it cost them to buy. Their policy decimated both the small retailer and their suppliers. I wonder if they realize that, with the continuing reduction in labour requirements or the sourcing of work outside of the UK, there will be nowhere their customers will be able to earn a wage to enable them to shop at all.

Today we have only one large-scale breeder of turkeys in this country; this was a British firm who beat the Americans with their breeding skills, only to be bought out by an American company. They supply breeding stock to selected multipliers to produce the commercial poults. These day-olds then go to people skilled in rearing them to six weeks old and after that they go to rear/fatteners, where they are put into environmentally-controlled houses, which look after everything they need with automatic feeding from large outside silos. These will be refilled on a regular basis by lorries, which blow the food into the silo. The air for the houses will be filtered, heated or cooled as needed and blown into the house, which will be light controlled. A standby generator will be on site, as a loss of supply would be fatal. To make these costly houses earn their keep, they are filled with many more birds than can be reared to sixteen weeks. When they are eight weeks old, the lorry arrives to take a load (possibly 1500) to the factory for killing. Now there is plenty of room for another two weeks' growth. At ten weeks another load is taken, not so many this time. This is repeated at twelve and at fourteen weeks, and then at sixteen weeks the house is emptied. This gives a wide weight range and produces quality meat, albeit without a great deal of flavour. Turkey meat is ideal, being high in protein, yet far lower in fat than any other poultry. It also is very suitable for serving with spices and sauces. When we were on a farm visit to Israel in the late Seventies, we called in at a restaurant for lunch. On the menu were schnitzels, which most of our tour ordered. When they were halfway though the meal, I asked, 'How do you like your turkey?' Nobody would believe they were eating turkey and I had to ask the chef to come out and show them it was turkey!

Three weeks is allowed for the litter to be taken out and the house and its surroundings cleaned. The building will be pressure hosed, all the equipment will be taken out, cleaned and disinfected, and any maintenance will be carried out. New litter will be put in and every thing assembled ready for the next batch of six-week-old youngsters, and it all starts over once more. With this time scale, three batches a year can be produced from one house, giving 20,000 saleable turkeys. Great care has to be taken with all aspects of this type of production or losses can be heavy.

CHAPTER 13

Breeding Turkeys

EARLY ON I WROTE about keeping turkeys in the wood and the trouble we had. Another problem was the torn backs of the laying hens, which was caused by the males while mating. If they were to slip, their toenails would rake the hen's back and sides, sometimes ripping the skin. To counter this, father managed to obtain canvas from Wellington bomber engine covers. Mother converted these into 'saddles', which had tapes to hold them in position. The tape slipped over each wing holding it in place. It covered the back and both sides, from the wing down to the tail. The canvas had been treated to make it waterproof for the job it had been designed for, but it was not too pliable and mother's Singer sewing machine didn't take kindly to it. As it was also treadle-operated, it was quite hard work. We didn't dare ask how long before tea would be ready when she was doing this job. These worked very well for the hens, but they were a little slippery for the stags and, unless they could balance, they could not copulate and therefore the eggs were not fertile.

In the meanwhile, father had approached Edney Bros., who manufactured shop blinds and had a factory at Boxmoor, near Hemel Hempstead, to see if they could undertake the manufacturing of these from new material. This they were able to do for us. They also made improvements which involved hemming all round the outside to stop fraying. To help the stags from slipping, a piece of cord enclosed in tape was fixed both sides of the saddle where it curved down the side of the hen. These worked very well and were sold to most turkey

Turkey hens with canvas saddles.

breeders. When Edney's closed down, a firm of sail makers in
Norfolk took over the manufacturing.

When the farm stopped breeding chickens, we were able to
bring the turkeys down from the wood to the old poultry pens.
The divisions had been removed and the area covered with
straw. Wattle hurdles were placed in the pens, with the object of
giving places where mating could go on without attracting the
unwanted attention of other males, who would try to take over.
Nest boxes with gates that prevented two or more birds occupy-
ing one nest were very successful. All were made on the farm.

Breeding turkeys was my pleasure. I found a great sense of
achievement in selecting, in the keeping of records and in
tracing the pedigree of birds we used for breeding. It was in the
early 1960s that we started a breeding programme. During this
period the Americans had a breed of turkey they called Baby
Beef. These birds carried much more meat on the breast than

A breeding pen in 1951.

any turkeys in this country. Unfortunately, no imports were allowed into England, to prevent any importation of disease. However, in Scotland they were allowed to import, and a number of people did. One was the Duchess of Kintyre and we bought stock or eggs, I am unable to recall which, from her. What I do remember, however, is a disagreement I had with Father over which male birds I could keep for our trap pens. (A trap pen is a breeding pen in which the birds could enter the nest box, which were individual, but had to be manually let out.) These birds were all numbered and this number would be marked on the egg. These eggs were hatched in small cages in which only eggs from one hen were placed. On hatching, they were given a wing band with the line number and also a number that was only relevant to that poult. Record keeping had to be first class, and there was only one maxim. *If in doubt throw it out.*

Bird-operated nesting boxes.

We had a broad breast male that my father thought would be unable to copulate properly, while I felt it was a risk worth taking because of the increased meat potential. He, however, was adamant that it would cause problems. I grumbled to Mother about it, and there must have been some 'pillow talk', as I was allowed to breed from that bird. In a few years' time every bird on the farm could be traced back to that one bird. However, Father's point was also proved, as the fertility of the flock started to decline. This affected the flock poult per breeding hen, which dropped each year. When we were only producing poults from April to June, the poults per breeder averaged forty-seven. To try to counteract this fall, we would select from the hens that had produced most poults one year; the next year breast width and meat characteristics would be chosen. This had a seesaw effect and was corrected when we changed over to all white turkeys.

We also found that we had more 'dead in shell'. (This is an egg in which the embryo had completed its development but failed to get out of the shell). We enlisted the help of an ADAS (Agricultural Development Advisory Service) embryologist at Weybridge, who discovered that, in a large number of the eggs, the poult had a parrot beak and short 'long bones' (legs). The parrot beak meant it was impossible for the poult to break the shell. The normal beak has a small hard horn attached to the tip of the top bill, which acts as a chisel to cut through the shell. This drops off during the first twenty-four hours of the poult's life. The long bones were half their normal length and therefore were not folded, making it impossible for the poult to rotate itself within the shell. The cause was a simple resistive gene, which meant that both male and female had to be carriers. By trap nesting and recording, we were able to identify both male and female carriers. These carrier males were mated with unknown females, and carrier females with unknown males. This showed up any of the unknown birds that carried the recessive gene, allowing us to use the birds that had been proved clear the following year, and so rebuild our pedigree flock.

This work was to be of no avail within eight years, as the bronze bird naturally had dark stubs (pin-feathers). If damaged these would discolour the skin, looking like a bruise. In addition, when the birds were plucked, if any un-plucked stubs were left, you would be told that you had not made a good job. With a white-feathered bird, you would not see if a few stubs had been left. It was during the late Fifties that white turkeys started to be the preferred feather colour and in the early 1960s we changed over to white birds. About this time Miss Cooper, of the Animal Health Trust, was developing artificial insemination of turkeys. She toured the country demonstrating the technique. We set about learning how to do this simple technique and eventually most of the birds in the country were produced this way.

We examined the semen under a microscope from all of the males used for breeding at the start of the season, to check that it was viable and of good quality. We did not need saddles for the hens, there was no fighting among the breeding males and, more to the point, fertility shot up, resulting in many more poults per hen. We would inseminate on Mondays and Thursdays in the late afternoon, as most hens would have laid their eggs by that time. Males were 'milked' each time but the hens were only inseminated every ten days.

There were three in our team: one to empty the nest boxes of birds and divide the pen in half with two hurdles. The hens were driven into a catching crate in one half. While this was being done the other two would be milking the males. Only enough males were milked at a time to provide the amount of semen required for each pen. Then the catcher would collect a bird and expose the oviduct to the inseminator. He would hold the tube that held the semen in the palm of his left hand with his thumb over the opening, both to protect and keep the semen warm. In his right hand was a hypodermic syringe with a piece of rubber catheter into which a short length of plastic tube was fitted. He would draw three millimetres of semen into the tube to introduce into the oviduct. For each hen a new plastic tube was used to prevent cross-contamination. The insemination process was carried out with the team working kneeling down. This kept any stress on the birds to the minimum. By handling the birds every ten days, we were able to remove any birds that had stopped laying, and arrange for them to be processed instead of needlessly feeding them for no return.

It was at the Smithfield Show that we saw white turkeys produced by W. R. Rose from Scotland. These had a very good confirmation and weight. We ordered 500 day-olds from him and from those birds we started to form our 'egg line' of white turkeys. We based this on the 'Bosset system', which we adapted to our needs as follows. We built sixteen folds, each holding four birds in individual runs within the one fold, complete with a nest box-come-sleeping area. The roof of this slid to allow the collection of the eggs and was marked with the dam's number, which also had to be written on the egg. Food and water were at the front. Four further folds were constructed much higher and without the nest-box, to accommodate the males to be housed two to a fold in their own run. We numbered from ten to eighteen, twenty to twenty-eight etc. the first number being the line number, the second the bird number. The males also had a line number. After the first year the male birds moved up one number i.e. the male from line one would be mated to line two hens. In year three, line one would be mated on line three hens. The hens always returned to their line number folds. In year eight, when the males would have been mated to their own line, they skipped that line and moved up two lines. This ensured that no siblings were mated. These hens were in their second year of production, while the male was in its first year. These folds were moved every third day.

Each bird had a record sheet that recorded eggs set, those infertile, dead germs, number hatched, any killed at hatching and why. It also noted the wing band number that was attached to each poult. These were also recorded in a wing band book, which could be used at selection time out in the pens. All losses were recorded on the hen's record. Once we had a bird producing five poults a week. They grew fast, but only lived five days. As they all died it did not matter, but if a number had lived and had been bred from, the losses they could have eventually caused, without pedigree work, would have been great.

In their first year these birds would have been in pens containing only full sisters mated to our large meat line. There would only have been two groups of sisters chosen from each line. This was the pressure we put on our selection. The hens produced from this cross were used for our commercial breeding flock, which in turn were mated to meat line males. The eggs laid per pen were recorded for these sister pens and only those from the best of the pair would be used to go into the grandparent pens.

We were able to buy, from Brian Dale near Ludlow, heavy broad white male turkeys for our meat line. However, when he decided to stop breeding, he kindly sold us the poults from his last hatch. From then on our flock was closed and we were breeding the meat line as well. Our criteria for this line were meat, balance and weight gain. We knew that the egg production would be low. However, so long as they carried a lot of breast meat, could walk well and carry themselves without being front down, we accepted the low poult production.

It had been suggested that one could trap for just twelve weeks, and in that time it was possible to collect enough records to enable selection of the correct birds to be made. After five years we found that you had to trap for the total length of time that the flock was expected to be in lay. We found that some birds would stop production at fourteen weeks, even if the poult production had been excellent up to twelve weeks. The time we were expecting the flock to lay was twenty weeks, which meant we could have kept birds for six weeks for no poults. It was also thought that one could change the male and in four weeks all poults would be his progeny. We tested this out by using a bronze male on white hens and we then changed to white males. This new mating would give bronze and white poults and we found it required nine weeks before the new cross was fully effective.

After fifteen years' breeding, we found that the egg line was only very slowly improving, so we started to trap the heavy line to improve their poult production. We had only been doing this for three years when we found the cost greater than we

The author and his father with white and bronze breeding males with
pedigree folds in the background.

could afford and started to buy our poult requirements from
Leacroft Turkeys. So ended my greatest enjoyment in turkey
farming.

CHAPTER 14

Turkey for the Table

WHEN WE FIRST started, nearly all poultry was sold through the butcher, who would buy his poultry Long Leg or New York dressed, both terms meaning that the bird had been plucked only. He would then, at Christmas, dress his shop with all the birds he had for sale. The outside would also be hung mainly with turkeys. You could choose your bird and your name would be tied on a tag around the neck. Then on 23 or 24 December, the birds would be gutted, ready for you to collect, along with bacon and sausages if you could afford these extras.

On the farm we would have all the birds hanging head first, to keep the blood in the cavity between the head and neck, so preventing the blood discolouring the skin. The butcher would come and haggle over the price. This was a true battle of wits, for the farmer and many of the butchers had no cold storage. The weather really ruled the price, though the consumer gained none of the reduction that the butcher enforced when the weather was mild.

My father always said 'a mild Christmas could ruin us' and 'it's a cruel mill when you're caught between the butcher and the weather.' Fortunately in the early 1950s more and more refrigeration became available. Had this not been so, today, with the mild Christmases we are experiencing, the butcher would soon ruin his poultry supplier.

In the early days all poultry would be hand plucked, the main object being to remove the breast feathers first and then pluck the legs, leaving about half an inch of feathers around the

117

leg joints, most of the neck feathers, most of the back and some long feathers on the wings. These were for protection when transporting. As long as the skin was intact and the bird was properly starved before it was killed, it would keep for up to three weeks with no refrigeration. If the feathers were not pulled in the correct direction, however, you could so easily tear the skin. You were not pulling one feather at a time but handfuls. Any tears would be sown up with a needle and white cotton, in the hope that it could not be seen.

Ducks and geese were much harder to pluck, as they had to be plucked twice, once to remove the feathers, then again to remove the down. It was then the butcher's job to do the final plucking and gutting. The poultry of this period did not have the meat or the weight of today's birds. In fact, seen against the broad breast now available, you would not be able to sell any of them! In the 1940s and 1950s, a hen turkey would weigh around twelve pounds (five and a half kilos) and the male twenty-five pounds (eleven and a half kilos). Today, a hen can weigh twenty-eight pounds and a male over fifty pounds. Poultry was only served on a high day, a holiday or some special occasion, with turkey only at Christmas.

This was a problem we encountered when we produced the first turkeys to be hatched in February. They were ready for killing in September and nobody wanted to know anything about them. We eventually sold them very cheaply on Smithfield Market. As I've written earlier, this made us experiment with cold storage. At that time most cold stores were mainly used to store meat (lamb that was wrapped in a muslin cloth for transport from New Zealand) at the butcher or wholesaler. This did not stop the meat drying out and being less juicy than it should have been. Frozen meat was always considered dry and of poor quality. The biggest trouble was that there was no wrapping that was capable of preventing 'freezer burn' or areas of dried-out meat. We had heard that ICI

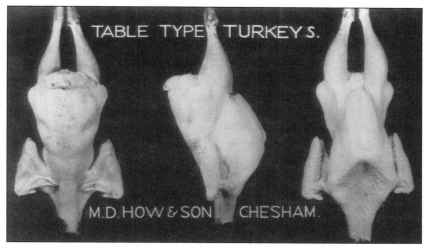

Turkeys for the table – early 1960s.

was producing polyethylene under the trade name 'Alkathine', a tubular film in rolls and in widths that increased by one-inch increments. I.C.I. granted us, and Petitts of Reedham in Norfolk, licences to convert this tubular film into bags. We were one of the first to be granted a licence. In retrospect it would have been more profitable if we had sold all the turkeys and converted the buildings into bag-making! There was no machinery to mass-produce bags at that time and, as we only required a low number anyway, we made our own. How we made these was to cut the film into the required length, lay them onto a curved piece of aluminum sheet, each sheet separated by a sheet of paper, until we had a pile of about twenty sheets. Another sheet of aluminum was then placed on top and weighted to hold them steady and then, with a sharp knife, we would cut the curve following the template. We used a Bunsen burner with which we would melt the plastic, so making the seal; the paper stopped the bags from fusing to each other.

Richard Roadnight, along with Ray Feltwell (the Oxford

ADAS poultry adviser) visited the farm to see what we were
doing. Seeing that we were using a vacuum cleaner to extract
the air from the bags, Mr Roadnight said he would send an
engineer from his factory in High Wycombe, to examine the
possibility of their manufacturing a more suitable tool for the
job. Within three weeks of the visit we had the first vacuum
pump to be used for removing air from turkey bags. This was
on a trolley with the pump attached to the base. A pipe rose to
six feet and there was a U-bend and a spring-loaded valve over
which the bag was held with the left hand whilst one's right
hand supported the bird. When the air was out, we gave a quick
spin and the bag was ready for sealing. This was achieved by
Sellotape around the twisted bag, tight to the bird. The extra
bag was removed and the stub pressed against a hot iron plate
heated by the Bunsen burner. You have to improvise when you
are the first!

The first turkeys were stored loose in racks, which was
adequate for a few hundred birds but no good for more. Firstly
it was difficult to find the weight you wanted and more worry-
ing was that the bags were damaged, which in turn allowed
'freezer burn' to appear on the birds. It was felt that the best
way around this would be to box them in cardboard cartons.
We wrote the weight on the outside and stacked them from
floor to ceiling. We found that by having a layer of five boxes,
three side-by-side and two end on, and alternating the layers,
we could go twelve layers high, sixty birds per stack, placed on
a stand allowing air to pass underneath.

We found Eburite Containers, box makers, who were willing
to make us the first turkey box. It came in a flat pack and we
had to make the box up, folding the flaps to make the bottom,
which were fastened with two-inch gummed paper on a roll.
The bird was placed inside and packed around with shredded
paper. This was perfectly adequate for stacking small weights
and for short travelling distances. As greater weights came

along, it was found that the bird would drop out of the bottom of the box. This did not impress Mr Justin of Sainsbury's when he was carrying one in a street in London and the bird dropped out. Not one of ours I'm glad to say. The answer was found by having an insert of cardboard that covered the bottom, thereby spreading the weight over the whole bottom instead of a weak point, at the centre. Today's boxes incorporate this along with two extra ends that strengthen the box for stacking.

A friend of mine, John Harrison, had just started his own business, 'Packaging Design', and he designed both our label and the wording on the box CHESSOVALE FLAVOUR FULL TURKEY. CHESSOVALE (our registered trademark) and FLAVOUR were in red, while FULL and TURKEY were blue. This remained unchanged during all our years of trading.

It was interesting that when we were looking for someone to build a small cold store for us, J. & E. Hall, who were king-pins among the refrigeration engineers at the time, would not quote for the job, as no one in their right senses would want to freeze turkeys! We found a small company in Bedford, Bedford Refrigeration, who undertook the job, but they would not put in a plant that would work at -5°F. All we could get was a box with four inches of cork insulation capable of +16°F. They insisted on having an airlock fitted, and we insisted that they refrigerated it and we used it to hang the birds when they had been killed. The refrigeration equipment was by Presscold of Oxford.

To freeze the birds quickly we purchased a chest freezer, to which we had a much larger compressor fitted to do the freezing of the oven-ready birds. This would freeze 500 pounds in twelve hours, which meant thirty birds per day on average. These were then transferred to the store, which we found we could make run at +10°F. for storage. With this setup we were able to cope with the early-hatched birds.

The fact that turkeys were still in short supply at Christmas enabled us to insist that part of any order had to be taken frozen. In fact, we found that most of the customers who gave birds away to their own customers and/or staff had had a much easier time, with no trouble keeping them for two or three days and transporting them around the country. They had no complaints and asked to have all their order frozen when ordering the next year. **Thus began the Frozen Turkey Industry.** From then on we started to see other people coming into the industry, John Lintern at Hoppers Farm, Holmer Green, being one of the first. We had a letter from him when he was a rep for Full-o-Pep, a poultry feed company, saying how pleased he was with his first forty day-old poults and could he double his order for next year. We supplied him as he built up his turkey enterprise, but before long, he wanted many more than we could supply and, as Father would not rely on just one customer, John had to look elsewhere. Later in 1962 he joined forces with Rupert Chalmers Watson from Fenton Barns, Scotland and Hugh Arnold from Hockenhull, to form British United Turkeys, which was big enough to operate large-scale genetic programmes and, over the years, they grew to be THE breeding farm to the world. Unfortunately, it is now American owned. A young employee of John's, Mr Ron Parsons, was still at Hoppers Farm when he retired a few years ago. Under the joint management they developed Hoppers Farm as a breeding farm and a hatchery unit, supplying breeding stock to others who became multipliers. BUT would provide so many females of one line and the required number of males from another line, similar to our own breeding programme. Being very much larger, they were able to run many, many more lines than we could. Eventually they could supply breeding stock from small birds for the retail trade up to large birds for catering. They had ten such sites spread over the country, which enabled them to run a rotation of emptying a site completely to prevent any build-up of health

A 'flavour full' turkey.

problems. By supplying breeding stock in this way they were able to protect their stock from being bred by others, in that they never supplied pure-line stock outside their own enterprise.

We increased our breeding flock to just over 500 hens to meet the demand. It was soon after this that *Eggs*, the forerunner of *Poultry World* carried a photo of Father with the caption 'Keep 500 Breeding Turkeys and pay Surtax.'

The Christmas gift trade, where firms gave a frozen oven-ready turkey, allowed for easy handling and played a large part in our Christmas market for very many years. Some orders were for two hundred and more. Before this, poultry was often seen on trolleys at mainline stations, in plaited rush carrier bags, their legs sticking out at one corner of the stitched up bag. What they were like on arrival I dread to think. They then had to be eviscerated and cleaned up and, if they arrived late, as they could, there would be no Christmas Dinner. Not a good advert for the firm giving them to their best customers!

Many family butchers switched to our oven-ready frozen birds. They were able to buy the weights they wanted and, where they had cold storage, were also able to buy cheaper than at Christmas. This early selling/purchase of turkeys brought in a much needed cash flow when our feed costs were at their highest. Ray Feltwell came up with the idea of killing the stags at twelve weeks of age and cutting them in half, so that they could compete with the chicken that had started to be readily available. Unfortunately, there were no trays or suitable packing marketed at the time, and the presentation was very poor. Chickens were not being cut up yet awhile, and the housewife did not like to see the raw bone inside. This was a project ahead of its time, before the public were ready, and it took many years work, promoting cut-ups, before portions were accepted.

The main people in the turkey industry, who kept plodding away, trying to make the British public accept that a turkey or a chicken when jointed was just the same principle as cut-up beef, pork or lamb, were Mike Warman and his wife, who could be found promoting turkey joints in many London stores. The old saying 'There's none so queer as folks' certainly was true in this instance. It took very many years before the public accepted that a joint was the way for small families to enjoy turkey. It was not until the 1980s, when Bernard Matthews launched his turkey roll, that portions really took off. It was quite by chance that we launched our own 'portioned' turkey on the same day. We had no prior knowledge whatsoever but, of course, his ability to advertise his product widely had a big knock-on effect for us.

Turkey portions.

Our first offerings were 'breast roll, fillets, slices of breast meat, drumsticks, thigh roll, wings, cubes of both white and dark meat, and mince.' When a customer called we would pull out a trolley with eight compartments containing a selection for them to choose from. This was not ideal but it enabled us to test the market before we had to spend more on an unproven project.

It was my daughter Margaret and son-in-law Henry who worked so very hard at this project, and I was very pleased that it went very well. They walked miles pushing leaflets through doors, selecting roads in Amersham, Chesham and Berkhamsted, making sure that all houses received a leaflet with prices and directions to find us. They also gave talks to the W.R.V.S., women's clubs and local shows. The biggest problem was convincing people that, although it was frozen, it would still have flavour.

The mass production and cost-cutting meant that the birds were killed, eviscerated, then cooled in tanks of flake ice for twenty-four hours, during which time they absorbed water, as opposed to the traditional method where the bird was hung entire, for up to a week or more before evisceration. Poultry cannot be frozen until rigor mortis has taken place and left, hence the need to store for twenty-four hours prior to freezing. The lack of flavour caused by this method was the biggest problem that we encountered. Customers could not understand why we wanted fresh price for a frozen article as frozen poultry was well known to be tasteless

It was Margaret and Henry's project, and something I had not done before. I made a point of not learning how to cut a bird up. It went so well that we had to build a new processing room complete with its own cold store and chill room. The point of sale had to have more room. Here we stopped boxing the whole turkeys in the room next to the cold store, took down the wall between our small waiting room, bricked up one of the doorways, lowered the ceiling and put in new fluorescent lighting, whose light wavelength was such that it enhanced the appearance of the meat.

We installed three ten-foot long display freezer cabinets, and a fresh (chill) display cabinet, a till that would record the type of sale, and a credit card machine. We also had a car park for ten cars, which could take more if needed, as it was at Christmas. We ended up offering a selection of over twenty items ranging from whole turkey, all the cuts possible, down to mince, three types of sausages and large and small burgers. Many cuts had sauces added to them and we also offered 'pet mince'. To make a profit, all of the turkey had to be sold. It was no good having a build-up of unsold items.

Margaret and Henry entered the NFU small business award

scheme, run in partnership with Marks & Spencer, and they reached the final six, from over thirty entries. The grading of our CHESSOVALE® brand of oven-ready turkey was very high. Any with the smallest blemish would be downgraded but these could now be used for cut-ups, which was a big saving.

I know of no-one else who is producing or ever produced the range of cut-ups we did. It is very pleasing to meet old customers who say how much we are missed, and who ask if there is anybody or anywhere they can find a supplier. So out there is a demand for high-quality cut-up turkey products. All our trading was based on top quality. If there was the slightest doubt about any of our products, it was discarded. 'If in doubt, throw it out.' It was not even used for pet food.

Turkey, after all, is a game bird, and no cook worth her salt, at any of the big houses on the estates, would dream of cooking a pheasant before the first maggot dropped on her head, from where they were hanging in the game room. The EC, with the legions of rule makers working in Brussels, would have put an end to that. They had decreed that poultry must be killed, de-feathered, and eviscerated in a continuing process and stored below 4°C. When the rules were first being formulated, as game birds were shot, they would have had to be de-feathered and eviscerated immediately. This has been the type of thinking we have had to endure for years. A great deal of time was spent in explaining that not everybody wanted this, and some concessions were won. The rules now apply to all poultry, at plants that process 10,000 and more birds per year. Our plant was approaching 20,000 per year. You can imagine what a strain it put on us, having to reduce staff and having no use for half our buildings. We applied for planning permission to convert buildings into small business units, but this was turned down, even when it was the governmental policy to allow diversifica-tion. This and the fact that supermarkets were using turkey as a loss leader made our size of unit unviable, and we sold the

A white male turkey.

farm and retired on 31 January 1999. So ended a lifetime in the turkey industry.

The turkey industry seems to have polarized over the last two years in that the smaller producer is now concentrating on dry-plucked birds for Christmas and leaving frozen to Bernard Matthews. Production of turkeys has dropped from 34.21 million birds in 1997 to 23.53 million birds in 2002; unfortunately a lot of this reduction has been made up with imports from Brazil, Italy and other countries at the cost of British jobs and British birds produced under British control. But as always you get what you pay for! On that sad note I will close, hoping you have enjoyed reading about my life and the turkey industry. I have met many people over the years and have enjoyed the camaraderie that exists among the turkey producers of this country. Some of my friends in the business have contributed their thoughts and these are included on the following pages.

Treasured Turkey Years

Memories of people who worked in and helped to form the industry.

IT WAS A GREAT privilege to serve as the executive secretary of the British Turkey Federation from 1973 to 1982, the years when feed prices doubled as a result of the catastrophic failure of the Russian harvest in 1972, the Poultry Meat Hygiene Regulations threatened the very existence of the NYD trade, as it was then known, and a charismatic Frenchman thought he would demolish the British turkey industry by supplying the whole of the UK market from Brittany; years when five-day drinking contests were held at the Grand Hotel in Eastbourne in February and were called National Conferences; when the likes of Dad's Army auctioned the heaviest turkeys for charity and Douglas Bader accepted the proceeds; when we presented Christmas turkeys to Prime Ministers, and much more. These are memories I treasure.

Ernest Magog, October 2003

The British Turkey Industry is one of the success stories of British Agriculture, non-reliant on government subsidies. Turkeys were imported into England early in the sixteenth century by a Yorkshire man, William Strickland of Boynton Hall, and by 1555 records show that you could buy turkeys on London markets. The real growth of the turkey market started to develop in the mid-1950s and by 1960 the frozen oven-ready market started to be established, with Christmas being the main market. However, Easter was developed with the mini turkey, followed by spring bank-holiday and August bank-holiday, so now a year-round business was being built. With the development of the cut-up turkey and added-value product, turkey was now within the reach of all people as a value-for-money buy.

The British Turkey Federation, of which I was chairman for seventeen years, (and later Chairman of the British Poultry Meat Federation) was the producer/hatchery of ideas. In the mid 1970s over £1 million was raised from producers towards generic advertising (something unheard of in British Agriculture) with TV, PR and press.

In these early days we were all pioneers. The friendship and sharing of knowledge were the keys to success. In 1960 there were one million turkeys but in 1996 there were thirty-five million from over 4,000 producers. The industry today is made up of large producers, with a small band of traditional farm-fresh, and imports from countries overseas, which have reduced the production in the UK.

It is my pleasure to have played a part for over forty years in this great industry and to have worked with a great set of people in an industry where large and small worked together to make the turkey the real value-for-money bird for all seasons.

Raymond W. Twiddle, OBE

I started in the industry in 1945 as a trainee at Y. Watanabe's Pedigree Breeding farm in Surrey where I trained for five years in between going in the army for National Service. Following this I had various poultry jobs in broilers etc. before joining Buxted Chicken Co. Then I went to Nitrovit as a poultry adviser and later specialised in turkey, finishing as the National Turkey Manager. After the sale of Nitrovit, I was transferred, as a poult salesman, to Ross Poultry, which was eventually amalgamated with Twydale Turkeys, where I became the National Poult Sales Manager until I retired in 1994.

During my turkey career, I was on the BTF Council

representing the feed trade. I was also a member of the Anglian Turkey Association. I was chairman for two years and have served on the committee for various periods, during which time I have received the Goodchild Trophy, the Allan Whipp Award and several cups from the ATA.

I started a Turkey Exchange for the ATA, when I discovered that producers were ringing everybody in the Essex area either looking for or selling weights they did not have. I suggested we operate an agency so that one person could be at the end of the phone and give information. I operated this from my office, with my secretary dealing with enquiries during working hours, after which I carried on from home. This proved successful and I was asked to carry it on. Last Christmas was our twenty-third year in existence and in that time we have helped to keep 313,000 turkeys off the market. After I retired I operated it as a business and formed my own company, Goodman Turkey Services, where I charge a registration fee to cover my telephone expenses.

On retirement I was also asked to become Secretary of the ATA, which has gone from strength to strength. When I took over, we were aiming for 100 members. This year we have topped 158. Obviously with this number of members from all over the UK, I am kept very busy organising speakers and functions. We have re-introduced the European trips every year in April and, with the help of BUT, have visited turkey farms and plants all over Europe, staying in Venice, Budapest, Barcelona, Prague, and Florence to date.

Len Goodman

My mother was the fourteenth child of a farming family, born in Thorne, Yorkshire. I had always wanted to marry a farmer and have a veterinary practice in our front room. It didn't work out like that. I came to London to join a news agency in 1963 and fell in love with the work of Christopher Bosanquet, then

MD of F J Lyons PR, who trained me up on Walls Handy Foods. I moved to George Hynes to handle British Bacon Curers' Federation, and via that to the Bacofoil Alcan industry. The marketing manager of Buxted Chicken in Sussex, Alan Toft, now the editor of *Pro Wholesaler*, discovered I wrote Pitmans shorthand and followed up on meetings and offered me my first contract PR job at £1,500 per year.

So Field Communications was born in 1971. When Buxted (Ross Foods) moved to Grimsby, he went on to trade journalism and his PA, Fran Webb, joined me. We worked out of a dingy office in Holland Road, London, rented to us for £10 a week by my former news agency editor, who was very proud of my move into consumer, fashion and food PR. Very soon Alan introduced us to the British Poultry Federation and the BTF hired us to handle their PR.

In the early 1970s, food and cookery journalism was in its infancy; we had no idea that cookery, which was rapidly disappearing from the school curriculum, would become a major leisure and entertainment business.

But the early BTF members began to understand that, if their industry was to grow, they must start cutting up the whole, large, Christmas turkey. Pioneers battled to pull the BTF members through the industry logistics, and marketing figures supplied by the growing market statistics industry were now considered at every marketing meeting.

Working in partnership with Ogilvie & Mather, the agency that had launched Bernard Matthews in his Norfolk suit with his wonderful Norfolk accent saying 'bootiful' on his first hugely successful TV commercials, the BTF launched a campaign called 'Turkey For All Seasons'.

It was a huge gamble to attempt to hold on to the enormous turkey Christmas market, whilst expanding turkey cuts, joints and the early further processed products into other times of the year, starting at Easter and going on to the other statutory bank-holidays when family and friends tended to get together. Co-funding was sought from products that sold 'on the back' of turkey meat, such as Ocean Spray cranberry sauces, Bacofoil, Alcan, Paxo, and other blue chip brands.

On the PR side, the Marketing Committee, then chaired by John Petrie of Dale Turkeys, decided on an 'open house' policy. I had the hard job of telling the committee that investigative journalism would continue and grow, and that consumer opinion would be steered by both print and electronic media. We had to police our own industry and to be as helpful as possible to all journalists.

No other industry could have hosted such a series of charismatic 'press events'. Turkey farmers, small and large, opened their doors. Years before, when I had launched Walls Popular Sausage, Christopher Bosanquet insisted we did it in a City of London Livery Hall – the Grocers Hall, if I remember correctly. Now, I took that lesson to heart and we decided to use the homes of turkey farmers, and ensure that any London events were as splendid as we could afford to make them. Roast turkeys were heralded into the Café Royal with a swirl of Scottish pipes, BTF conferences were held in the best of regional locations such as The Grand at Eastbourne (rather like today's party political rallies) and major supermarket buyers flocked to attend BTF events at Searcy & Tansley behind Harrods.

At the heart of the BTF were the turkey farmers who had moved into processing, and most of them were family businesses at the start. Even the larger processors, such as Twydales, Matthews and Sun Valley, were still run by the originators. I recall Tim Denham Smith, with his matinée idol good looks, cooking turkeys at a high temperature and carving them so proudly to show food and cookery writers the juices slipping invitingly down the breast meat. Brian Dale welcomed the press in with panache and style, his family and friends having prepared an amazingly tempting buffet of turkey and salmon with little fishes 'swimming' up the aspic jelly. Raymond Twiddle, after a hard conference, was 'chaired' round the room. He and Enid gave generous hospitality to media and to us foot-soldiers in their magical manor house in Yorkshire. Ron How's amazing footwork on the conference dance floor enraptured all the turkey wives around. I still remember his somewhat bemused smile when we tried to introduce a campaign that he had thought of twenty years ago.

I also recall Tony Burlton and Dot, sitting with Molly and Derek Kelly, Mike and Mary Warman and me in Birmingham one year, Mary displaying a pair of Mike's new underpants, and a large part of the formal conference dinner evaporating into a lot of female giggling. June Funnell was always with us and, whilst appearing to be shocked by our raunchy style, always enjoyed the conferences whilst handling the enormous amount of hidden dross.

Ernest Magog was in my view the best general secretary the BTF ever had, full of fun, dedication, and able to read between the lines. After one major seven-hour meeting, Ernest and I came into High Holborn tube station saying, 'Thank God we got through that session.' Suddenly there was a call from behind us. It was John Petrie saying, 'Hello. Now, about the latest marketing statistics...' We all laughed and went to the nearest pub.

I remember, too, the statesmanlike stance of Rupert Chalmers Watson, his stately wife and son and trips across the Scottish countryside in four-wheel drives. Happy days.

Why should the consumer media cover turkey meat at times other than Christmas and the major bank-holidays? We decided to create recipe dishes with this delicious, nutritious and very versatile meat for 'everyday' or weekend cooking. Home economists Rosemary Wadey and Marguerite Patten, now OBE and the doyenne of cookbook writers, worked hard to move the concept of turkey meat into a more popular language, while Molly Kelly busily cooked whole turkeys upside down.

Derek Blunden, then with Twydale Turkeys, helped me coin the word TOSCAS, and the first media awards were born. TV luminaries such as Michael Barry, OBE, and Patrick Anthony helped us build the excitement and interest around the industry marketing efforts. Turkey roasts and cuts were featured regularly on the emerging TV food and cookery programmes. We linked heavily with Ocean Spray cranberry sauce, telling the story of the Pilgrim Fathers and the first American Thanksgiving Dinner which formed the basis of an ongoing educational programme that ran for years and gathered yet more TV and news media coverage.

Now, twenty-five years later, my PR consultancy is still working for the Ocean Spray Cranberry Co-operative. The UK is the next largest market for cranberry products outside the USA.

Gina Field, October 2003

(Gina Field is chairman of Field McNally Leathes Ltd., a specialist food and drink PR and marketing consultancy, which handled the BTF account in the 1970s and 1980s and whose expanded food team is back looking after the British Turkey Meat campaign.)

I count myself very lucky in my choice of career on leaving Reading University in 1963. I had the opportunity to join the largest UK feed company but instead chose to join British United Turkeys Ltd, a recently formed turkey breeding company which very few people at that time had heard of. British United Turkeys is now the world's largest primary turkey breeding company, whereas the UK feed industry has gone through numerous mergers and reorganisations.

Not only was the choice of company fortuitous but the

turkey industry, which at that time was in its infancy, turned out to be one of the most dynamic sectors of agriculture in the last forty years. At its peak in 1995, it was in excess of fifteen fold its size in 1963. Unfortunately, since that time, it has been regressing but the signs are that this has been halted and some recovery can be expected.

Since the early 1950s, turkey production had been almost a licence to print money. The market was based around Christmas and the turkey was priced as a luxury meat. Several technical advances occurred in the late 1950s, which laid the foundation of the modern turkey industry. Probably the most important was the ability to freeze the turkey carcasses so that they could be produced throughout the year for sale at Christmas. The advent of artificial insemination enabled large-scale breeding programmes to be established and the increased knowledge of the influence of daylength on reproduction enabled all the year breeding and supply of poults to take place.

The high profitability of the industry in 1963 meant the introduction of an impecunious student into a new and exciting world where money seemed no problem. This was best illustrated by the annual British Turkey Federation Conference held at the Grand Hotel, Eastbourne, which climaxed with a banquet, after-dinner speeches, entertainment by a TV personality and black tie dance.

However, reality took hold when eventually production exceeded demand and prices plummeted, which resulted in the evitable shake-out of the less efficient producers. This process of good prices followed by overproduction, poor prices and bankruptcies or mergers, has been repeated at intervals over the forty years. However, the overall trend was an expanding, vibrant industry.

A significant development was the move from marketing turkeys as whole carcasses to further processing the carcasses to produce joints of meat and then, later, sophisticated meat products and more recently, ready-to-cook dishes. The number of products on the supermarket shelves continues to expand. The main driving force for this has been Bernard Matthews Ltd. Its founder, Bernard Matthews, has been the dominant personality in the UK industry throughout the last forty plus years.

To be closely associated with the genetic progress and the expansion of its market share achieved by BUT has indeed been a privilege. British United Turkeys Ltd was the brainchild of Rupert Chalmers Watson of Fenton Barns Turkeys Ltd, Drem, North Berwick, in Scotland. He put together a consortium, which included Hugh Arnold of Hockenhull Turkeys Ltd., Tarvin, Cheshire, John Lintern of Hoppers Farm, Great Kingshill, Bucks., and George Nicholas of Nicholas Turkeys in California, USA. The latter must have ultimately bitterly regretted putting some of his blood-lines into the newly formed company, because the new company eventually challenged his own company around the world and after his death had a greater share of the world turkey market.

Rupert Chalmers Watson was a visionary and a larger-than-life character who was also involved in the start of the UK broiler industry and table egg business. Those of us who knew him have a store of anecdotes about him. He liked a drink and did not discourage his staff from partaking, but woe betide anyone who let the side down or was not present for the first lecture of the morning at a conference.

Hugh Arnold was the Breeding Director of BUT for thirty odd years and was very much a hands-on geneticist. He was blessed with an innate sense of how a turkey could be structured to carry the increasing weight without suffering subsequent leg problems. On retiring from BUT he has become a very successful breeder of Simmental cattle. The ultimate success of BUT was due to an unlikely partnership of Hugh Arnold and the arrival of 'Mo' Hawkins, a businessman recruited from Lyons, the tea and confectionery company. They had different strengths, one with turkey sense, the other with business strengths, which resulted in a profitable company with high ethics and a strong emphasis on what was right in the long term.

The company was ultimately bought by Merck, Sharpe and Dohme in 1978 and is now part of the Merial Group. It is still staffed by long-serving senior executives but with an influx of new blood waiting in the wings.

The genetic progress that has been made in the last forty years would have seemed incredible in 1963. At that time the male turkey weighed circa sixteen pounds in sixteen weeks and the female twelve pounds. Forty years later, the 'BUT Big 6' is almost exactly double the weight at sixteen weeks of age. The improvement in food conversion ratio is of the same order. The selection for growth rate is criticised by some welfare organisations. The large environmental benefit, which comes along with it in terms of reduced requirement for arable land and reduced manure production to produce the same amount of turkey meat, is overlooked.

The improvement in reproduction is similarly spectacular. In 1963 a good flock was one which laid sixty eggs per hen in twenty-four weeks with a hatch of eggs set around 60 per cent to 66 per cent. The 'BUT 8' parent hen of 2003 will lay on average around 124 eggs in the same period with a hatchability of eggs set around 85 per cent or almost 300 per cent of the offspring of forty years ago. The health of today's turkey is extremely good, with all known egg transmitted diseases, particularly the mycoplasmas, eliminated, although re-infection from chicken or wild pheasants is an ever-present risk.

What then of the future? At first sight it is difficult to be optimistic because of the threat of imports from low-cost countries with emerging industries, such as Brazil and Chile. However, there are grounds for optimism. The cost of producing red meats should rise considerably faster than the cost of producing turkey meat. The reason for this is the progressive withdrawal of subsidies for agriculture, which has helped keep red meat prices low and arable prices high. Turkey feed costs should therefore be lower and competing red meat sales prices higher. Genetic progress will also be faster with turkeys than sheep and cattle, with their longer generation interval and fewer offspring. The consumption of turkey meat should recommence its upward curve. There are also aspects, which could make it more difficult for imports e.g. the cost of transport, legislation on welfare etc. The development of niche markets based on local breeds should also continue to develop.

The current generation of new entrants to the industry will be extremely fortunate if they have such a stimulating and exciting career as I have had in the turkey industry.

Dr Cliff Nixey

I believe that I first met the author on a regular basis when, as National Poultry Meat Specialist for ADAS for the Ministry of Agriculture, I was invited to join the Turkey Growers Committee of which he was a member. I felt much at home, as I suspect that I had experienced many of the trials and tribulations of turkey production that they had all experienced.

In the late 1940s I was working on a general farm and hatching and selling goslings (eggs 2/-; day-old goslings 10/-) and rearing table poultry for sale to local hotels as a sideline to get extra cash. At around this time I was invited by Tom Keen of Purly Park Hatchery at Reading to set up a duck, goose and turkey hatchery for him. This was a useful period as it enabled me to visit and select suitable flock farms. At the end of the season I decided that I needed more technical information and spent a year at Plumpton Farm Institute. I was particularly fortunate to be introduced to genetics by D.P. Hickinbotham (who later became Research and Development Director for the

Buxted Chicken Company) and this was most helpful when I undertook the management of the Duke of Bedford's poultry unit at Woburn in 1950.

I built up a 1500, pure-Sussex, breeding flock, selling hatching eggs, pure and first crosses, and I had a table poultry section, incorporating Indian Game for extra breast meat. I also set up a turkey-breeding section – improving egg production in the female line and breast width and growth in the male line. I came up against fertility problems, as breast width improved in the males. I had the turkeys sexed by Stan Watham, the first time that he had been asked to sex turkeys, which enabled me to caponise and feed the males separately for killing at sixteen weeks. All birds were sold 'long legged' either locally or direct to Smithfield market. (I seem to remember prices of 7s. 6d per pound for turkeys and 4s. 2d. per pound for chicken. Very lucrative!)

At the Poultry Research Unit at Houghton I was involved in a lot of experimental work. One area in which I had a particular interest, and with which I had earlier problems at the Duke of Bedford's farm, was the effect selection for breast width was imposing on the fertility of the male turkey, and over a five-year period I was very much involved with Doreen Cooper in the early work on the artificial insemination of turkeys, looking at various semen diluents and means of maintaining the viability of sperm. I also worked with the Low Temperature Research Centre in Cambridge on storage of poultry meat.

In the early 1960s, the Poultry Industry was changing dramatically and I was interested to work more closely with it. I joined a National Feed Company as Poultry Adviser, covering Dorset to Kent and north through Worcester and Oxfordshire. This gave me an opportunity to become more involved with larger-scale commercial enterprises. I was at the start of the expansion of the Buxted Chicken Company – both the broiler and breeder sectors – and with their Research Farm.

I worked with Cobb chicken, the Fatstock Marketing Corporation and other companies to establish flock farms and broiler groups. I also worked closely with various turkey enterprises including Southern Turkeys and Kingfeast Turkeys and helped to set up a marketing group with Romney Marsh Turkeys, besides covering feeding systems and various general ongoing management problems.

There was still much to learn about the Poultry Industry and when Dr Rupert Coles approached me to join what was then NAAS (the National Agricultural Advisory Service) in the late 1960s, I welcomed the chance, as it opened the door to research facilities and an excellent data retrieval system. I spent my first six months on poultry economics, followed by some county advisory work in Preston and was then promoted to National Poultry Specialist on poultry meat. Initially this was to encourage NAAS Advisors into improving their confidence/knowledge of broiler production as the industry had, in the main, increased faster than NAAS advisory ability. I spent my initial year looking at broiler group production targets which I continued to do in conjunction with Dudley Thomson of the NFU and later with Jim Holton, until I retired in the late 1980s. At this stage, with the retirement of Taffy Morgon, the previous NAAS turkey specialist, I added turkeys to my poultry meat list.

The old NAAS was renamed ADAS (Agricultural Development and Advisory Service) and with its research facilities at Gleadthorpe, a comprehensive series of experiments was mounted to examine temperature/diet/growth interactions within turkey and broiler growing. I disseminated the findings to the industries by talks and written articles, the larger-scale units and feed companies making the greatest use of the information.

Both the turkey and broiler industries had become highly efficient in producing meat for sale and it was decided that my role should move towards improving the quality of the produce and I was designated National Poultry Meat Quality Specialist.

Initially I set up, with Stafford College Catering Department, a quality assessment panel and invited both broiler and turkey companies to send their standard sales material in for examination. The birds were given marks for packaging, labelling information and appearance, as perceived by the housewife. Microbiological assessments were made, as were cooking losses (by gas and electricity) and the cooked birds were offered to a taste panel. The results were confidential. The best companies were given a signed certificate. I believe that the scheme gave valuable unbiased information. Follow up advice, if required, was given on site.

The most costly commercial loss is the downgraded bird loss of saleable meat, and I visited most broiler companies to examine their processing plants. Early in the 1970s I travelled to the Poultry Meat Symposium in Denmark and, in conjunction with representatives of the UK Veterinary profession and the Food Research Institute in Norwich, fought for the retention of the UK 'long legged' method of marketing poultry. I had many other behind-scenes activities – for example, to provide answers for parliamentary questions, to provide material for ministers' speeches, and to provide technical advice to ADAS regions and for the press. I also worked with the Agricultural Engineering Department at Silsoe, Beds., on automating broiler catching methods, and on the possibility of 'on-line' killing, using gas. I sat on the UN/ECE committee in Geneva to evolve international quality standards for poultry meat.

Having experienced for myself the vagaries of the plucking/holding period for long-legged birds prepared for the Christmas market and for subsequent storage by the customer, I was particularly interested in the time/temperature interactions on flavour/spoilage of poultry meat and set up a series of trials in order to examine the problem. I introduced Derek Kelly to Dr Geoff Mead of the Food Research Institute at Norwich, looking at flavour preferences by town and country consumers of turkeys on different lengths of storage times when the long-legged bird was hung, work requested by M. D. How, which confirmed their preference flavour with birds hung for six days at 40°C.

4° C

The Microbiologists and Meteorological Departments at ADAS, Wolverhampton, assisted me with work on the growth of spoilage organisms over time and accumulating variable winter storage conditions on un-eviscerated long-legged turkeys, either wet or dry plucked. I disseminated the findings by means of evening talks and written articles. I was also much involved with on-farm advice, for example, the effect of odours (disinfectants, wood shavings etc.) on poultry flavour, and the spoilage of poultry meat that occurred from processing, storage, delivery and customer abuse.

I have found putting these notes together a pleasant exercise, which has brought back a lot of memories.

J.A. Binstead, July 2003

Appendix II

A list of people who helped to develop the turkey industry.

Arnold, Hugh
Founder member of BUT. Breeding specialist. His selection of birds contributed greatly to the improvement of the meat production of turkeys.

Barnet, Peter
Secretary **BTF**.

Blount, Dr Percy
Veterinarian working for BOCM on poultry and turkeys in charge of the Stoke Mandeville experimental farm.

Bradley Bros.
Middle Wallop, Hampshire. Supplied Sainsbury's with frozen turkeys; later produced canned turkey but this did not catch on.

Bradnock, Peter
Secretary **BTF**.

Chalmers Watson, Rupert
Scotland. Proposed the formation of a **British Turkey Federation** at an Oxford meeting, where it was agreed to meet at Poultry Show at Olympia. Names and £5 put into box and the **BTF** was formed. Formed British United Turkeys Ltd in 1962 with Hugh Arnold and John Lintern.

Coles, Rupert
Head of the poultry section of the Ministry of Agriculture, Fish

& Food. Always wore a red carnation in his buttonhole. Retired to Malta.

Cook, Phil
Started Leacroft Turkeys. Won heaviest turkey a number of times with weights in excess of eighty pounds.

Cooper, Doreen
Research worker at Houghton poultry research station; toured country teaching the method of inseminating turkeys.

Dorran, Eileen
Secretary **BTF**.

Dring, Reginald
First Secretary of **BTF**.

Feltwell, Ray
Oxfordshire Poultry advisory officer; wrote a book on turkey farming.

Field, Gina
PR Officer for the **BTF** for many years.

Hawkins, Mo
Joined BUT as commercial director 1967.

How, M.D. Pre-war producer
Chesham, Bucks. (Bronze Turkeys) Experimental work and screening of drugs for the cure of 'blackhead' for Weighbridge and of supplements for turkeys. Member of Table Producers & Turkey committee of NFU. Founder Member of **BTF**. Council member for many years.

How, R.M.
Worked with father, M.D. How, producing the first early-

hatched turkeys; first freezing of turkeys on the farm. Discovered chondrodystrophy and bred it out of their strain of bronze turkeys. Supplied most of the turkeys given by **BTF** to the Prime Minister from Jim Callaghan to Tony Blair. Founder Member, and believed to be one of a very few surviving founder members, of **BTF**.

Kelly, Derek, MBE
Championed the smaller producer and free-range production of turkeys. Saved the Bronze turkey as a fine meat-producing bird. **BTF** member. Chairman of NFU Turkey committee.

Lintern, John
Gt. Kingshill, Bucks. One of first to produce turkeys on a large scale, processed on the farm and sold frozen. Helped to form BUT. Retired to South Africa.

Magog, Ernest
Secretary **BTF**.

Matthews, Bernard
Gt. Witchingham Hall, Norfolk. Bought airfields and used the runways as floors for his turkey barns; removed and sold lead from roof of Gt. Witchingham hall and replaced with corrugated iron. Lived in part and reared turkeys in other rooms. Grew to be the largest turkey enterprise in the world. President of **BTF**. Catchphrase: 'Bootiful.' Traded as Bernard Matthews Ltd since 1959. Has since brought Gt. Witchingham Hall back to its former glory.

Melville, Major (later) Colonel
Chesham, Bucks. Reared poultry pre-1939. Switched to turkeys during war. Allowed **BTF** to have their first office in the Bury, Chesham. Founder member of **BTF**. Produced turkey pies delivered to homes.

Motley, W.A. 1927. Pre-war Producer
Middle Wallop, Hampshire. Manager Frank Garwood. Kept all his breeding birds in folds. Incubated in corrugated iron sheds with gaps and on earth floors in the early days. Was one of the early turkey farmers. Great believer in fresh grass, which he claimed had a 'trigger factor' in the production of hatching eggs. (Bronze Turkeys). **BTF** member.

Murdock, Sheila
Editor and producer of *Turkeys* magazine.

Nixey, Dr Cliff
British United Turkeys Nutritionist. Did much work to raise the nutrition of turkeys.

Peel, Frank. Pre-war Producer
Norfolk. Bred Norfolk Black Turkeys pre-1939 and his grandson still breeds Norfolk Black.

Rose, W.R.
White Turkey Breeder, Scotland.

Smith, Mrs. Pre-war Producer
Monkton Court, Hampshire. (British White Turkeys). Member of T.P. & T. committee of NFU. Son Michael carried on for a number of years.

Snell A.E.
Helped to form Turkey Federation in Australia.

Twiddle, Raymond, OBE
Formed Twydale Turkeys Ltd. Chairman of **BTF** for many years.

Warman, Michael
One of the first to sell cut-up turkey. Goose Green.